Bhopal

Bhopal

Rahul Varma

Playwrights Canada Press
Toronto

Playwrights Canada Press
269 Richmond St. W., Suite 202, Toronto, ON M5V 1X1
phone: 416.703.0013
info@playwrightscanada.com • www.playwrightscanada.com

For professional or amateur production rights, please contact:
Kensington Literary Representation, 34 St. Andrew St., Toronto, ON M5T 1K6
kensingtonlit@rogers.com

Playwrights Canada Press acknowledges the financial support of the Government of Canada through the Canada Book Fund and the Canada Council for the Arts, and of the Province of Ontario through the Ontario Arts Council and the Ontario Media Development Corporation for our publishing activities.

Front cover artwork by Tracy Martin
Production Editor: JLArt
Hindi script on pages 69–71 courtesy Dr. Kamlesh Gupta.

Library and Archives Canada Cataloguing in Publication

Varma, Rahul
        Bhopal / Rahul Varma.

A play.
ISBN 978-0-88754-810-9

        I. Title.

PS8593.A74B46 2005   C812'.54   C2005-901615-9

First edition: April 2005
Second printing: July 2012
Printed and bound in Canada by Marquis Book Printing, Montreal

This play is dedicated to the victims of the Bhopal disaster.

Bhopal by Rahul Varma has been translated into Hindi as *Zahreeli Hawa* by Dr. Habib Tanvir. It was also translated into French by Paul Lefebvre.

TABLE OF CONTENTS

On the night of 3 December 1984, Union Carbide's pesticide plant exploded, engulfing the city in a billow of deadly poisonous fumes. Small children fell like flies, men and women vainly scurried for safety like wounded animals, only to collapse, breathless and blinded by the gas. By morning, the death toll was more than 500, by sunset, 2,500. By the following day, numbers had no meaning. That night, Bhopal became the largest peacetime gas chamber in history.

Union Carbide came to India in 1905 while the country was still under British rule. Until the night of the explosion, the company was best known for the manufacture of the Eveready battery. By the mid-60s the company had moved into agrochemicals, and by the mid-70s it had become one of India's largest manufacturers of chemical fertilizers and pesticides. The company's promotional film showed healthy green crops blowing in the wind, birds singing, and men, women and children beaming with happiness as the line scrolled across the screen: "Union Carbide will touch every life in India."

Union Carbide did indeed touch many lives in India: more than 20,000 people have died so far, more than 10,000 were seriously injured, 20,000 were disabled, and thousands have suffered the ravages of respiratory disease, madness, cancer, and other unidentified illnesses. The foundations for the explosion were laid in a corporate boardroom in the US and then shipped to India: the plan to mass manufacture Sevin Carbaryl, which would generate large quantities of a by-product called Methyl Isocyanate (MIC)—the most poisonous chemical known to man.

Long before this "accident" the effects of MIC were seen in nearby residents, who experienced diseases unknown to medical science, as well as in animals, which died near the company drainage pipe. When animals were found dead near the pipe, the company responded with cash. After this, it became a routine practice for animals that died of old age to be tossed into the effluent by their owners so they could collect compensation from the company. While the company succeeded in silencing the villagers about the "loss of their animals," MIC continued to make its way into the bloodstreams of the neighbouring people, with tragic effects. Women gav birth to deformed babies and infant mortality rose to alarming levels.

As environmental awareness and labour costs rise in the West, multinationals relocate their manufacturing operations to the Third World, where wages are ludicrously low and environmental regulations are virtually nonexistent. They do so by convincing the unpopular Third World states that poverty is their greatest environmental hazard. Mr. Warren Anderson, then chief of Indian subsidiary's parent company, put it succinctly when he said, "*Without the technology and the capital multinationals help to introduce, developing countries would have little hope of eradicating poverty and hunger.*" The MIC-based method of manufacturing Sevin Carbaryl was banned in Europe and the US—an example, it would seem, of the multinationals placing a higher value on Western lives than on lives in the Third World.

Public analysis of Bhopal in the US did little to lay the groundwork for the kind of change that will protect victims in the Third World from unequal treatment, dumping, negligence, and the callous behaviour of multinationals. For example, Dow chemicals, which bought Union Carbide in 2001, refuses to clean up the waterbed in Bhopal. The waterbed is contaminated with more than twenty known carcinogens. While governments, papers, Union Carbide's lawyers, and the company's new owner continue to speculate about who is responsible, the poor people of Bhopal have no choice but to live with poisoned water.

Bhopal is a vivid and painful reminder of corporate inhumanity, an example of callous mass murder legitimized in the name of progress, development, and the state. It does not grab the headlines anymore, but the Bhopal Syndrome lives on. Even after twenty years, mothers who inhaled poisonous gas on or after the explosion are giving birth to horribly deformed babies. While still in the womb, babies are inheriting unformed limbs, melted skin, and holes in their brain tissue. This is a fundamental attack on the God-given right of children to be born healthy and free from bodily harm.

In their death, the victims of Bhopal have given us a sense of awareness. Let no Bhopals happen anywhere in the world ever again.

Rahul Varma
Montreal, 1 September 2002

FOREWORD

Nineteen years ago, highly toxic Methyl Isocyanate (used in the manufacture of the insecticide Sevin) leaked from a Union Carbide factory in Bhopal, India, killing thousands of people while they slept, and poisoning hundreds of thousands more in what is now acknowledged as the worst industrial accident in history. The repercussions of this "accident" can still be felt. More than 20,000 people have died to date and an estimated 150,000 people continue to suffer from the long-term effects of gas exposure: reduced vision and cancer, as well as respiratory, neurological, and gynaecological disorders. Children of survivors are born deformed and endure severe menstrual disorders.

The Union Carbide site (at the centre of this populous city) remains contaminated. Chemical wastes continue to poison people living near the abandoned factory. Testing conducted by Greenpeace in 1999 found cancer-, brain-damage- and birth-defect-causing chemicals in the soil and groundwater in and around the factory site, at levels up to 50 times higher than US Environmental Protection Agency safety limits. Mercury levels were 20,000 to 6 million times higher than levels accepted by the World Health Organization. A 2002 study by the Fact-Finding Mission on Bhopal found traces of lead and mercury in the breast milk of nursing women.

Dow Chemical bought Union Carbide in 2001. Dow publicly claims to be "a leading science and technology company… committed to the principles of sustainable development" that "seek[s] to balance economic, environmental and social responsibilities." The company, however, has refused to accept any responsibility for cleaning up the Bhopal site, claiming they acquired only Union Carbide's assets when they bought the company, not its liabilities. In December 2002, when 200 survivors of the Bhopal disaster staged a protest at Dow Chemical's Mumbai head office, demanding that Dow take responsibility for cleaning the site, Dow responded by suing the protesters the equivalent of $10,000 US for "loss of work."

Dow Chemical isn't the first corporation to make grand claims about its mission and then behave with utter disregard for everything but its bottom line, and claims regarding the munificence of our intentions and the beneficence of Western technology are not new either. Warren Anderson, Union Carbide's CEO, for example, maintained years ago: "Without the technologies and the capital that multinationals help to introduce, developing countries would have little hope of eradicating poverty and hunger. In India alone it is estimated that pesticides alone save 10% of the annual food crop, enough to feed 70 million people."

Shortly after the Bhopal disaster, The *Wall Street Journal* argued, "It is worthwhile to remember that the Union Carbide insecticide plant and the people surrounding it were there for compelling reasons. India's agriculture had been thriving, bringing a better life to millions of rural people, and partly because of the use of modern agricultural technology that includes applications of insect killers..."

To what degree were these claims accurate or defensible?

Union Carbide and other companies that produced fertilizers, herbicides, and pesticides, were part of a massive effort during the 1970s and '80s known as the Green Revolution. This term described a movement that aimed to increase food yields by using new strains of food crops, irrigation, fertilizers, pesticides, and mechanization. The Green Revolution promised to harness the power of science, technology, and industrial development to tackle hunger in the developing or Majority World. Unfortunately, the promises of the Green Revolution were never realized.

While some increases in yields were seen (not as spectacular as initially hoped), the Green Revolution also increased the disparity between rich and poor farmers. Only wealthy farmers with large plots of land could afford and use the mechanized equipment required for this type of farming. These farmers displaced or evicted the sharecroppers who then crowded into city slums (such as the one surrounding the UC plant in Bhopal).

Furthermore, the high yield varieties promoted and grown during the Green Revolution (and today) did not feed the hungry. The Green Revolution favoured cereals, whereas the Majority World's poor typically eat peas, beans, and lentils. The "surplus" food the Green Revolution produced was exported to wealthy countries.

Business Week magazine noted, "even though Indian granaries are overflowing now," because of increased wheat and rice yields, "5,000 children die each day of malnutrition. One-third of India's 900 million people are poverty-stricken." And consequently could not afford to buy the "surplus" food. The World Bank noted in a 1986 report that simply increasing the amount of food available would not address the problem of hunger. Dealing with hunger would require "redistribut[ing] purchasing power and resources toward those who are undernourished." The Green

Revolution did the opposite. Moreover, it made even those farmers who could afford the growth it offered more dependent on foreign technology, chemical products, and machinery. (A little more than a decade ago, cotton farmers in Gujarat sprayed their cotton 6 to 8 times a year; today they spray 20 to 30 times a year).

Clearly, the claims made for Green Revolution technology were, at best, overstated, at worst, outright lies. Susan George, author of *How the Other Half Dies*, summed up the Green Revolution as "a complex system for foreign agribusiness domination of how, where, and what Third World farms will produce and at what cost." What then is the new agricultural revolution, the biotech version—trumpeted as the ultimate free market answer to hunger—but a complex system for agribusiness domination of the genetic structure of life?

If this assertion appears hyperbolic or hysterical, consider the more than 30 US patents on India's Neem tree, and on the indigenous knowledge about the tree's properties and uses. Consider the patents held by pharmaceutical firms Pfizer, Merck, and Bristol-Myers Squibb on various bacteria and fungi. Consider the $100 million earned annually by Eli Lilly from two drugs derived from the rosy periwinkle, a plant found only in the rainforest of Madagascar, which has received nothing in return for the plant's exploitation; consider the efforts to patent basmati rice, which has been cultivated for centuries by farmers on the foothills of the Himalayas. Finally, consider Monsanto's so-called "Terminator" Technology—the genetic modification of plants to prevent them from producing viable seeds. These bio-engineered plants "terminate" their own life cycles, preventing farmers from storing seeds and forcing them to return annually to Monsanto to buy more.

Of course, farmers aren't stupid. They can see through Monsanto's (and others') claims and pledges "to deliver high-quality products that are beneficial to our customers and the environment." Farmers in the Majority World have consistently resisted the introduction of these second wave Green Revolution products. In India, a campaign of civil disobedience, Operation Cremate Monsanto, has burned test fields of genetically modified crops. The world's largest agricultural research institute, the Consultative Group on International Agricultural Research (CGIAR), has banned "terminator technology" from their crop breeding programs. They refuse to incorporate any genetic systems designed to prevent seed germination because of "concerns over potential risks of its inadvertent or unintended spread through pollen; the possibilities of sale or exchange of inviable seed for planting; the importance of farm-saved seed, particularly to resource-poor farmers; potential negative impacts on genetic diversity, and the importance of farmer selection and breeding for sustainable agriculture."

These challenges to corporate attempts to control the basic building blocks of life are critical. However, the fight is an uphill one and the stakes and spoils are enormous, perhaps unprecedented. Atal Bihari Vajpayee, the former Prime Minister of India has proclaimed, "Biotechnology is a frontier area of science with a high promise for the welfare of humanity. [...] I am confident that the fruits of biotechnology would be harnessed for the benefit of millions of poor people as we move into the next millennium."

Unfortunately, history shows that, contrary to Vajpayee's optimism, it is the few very wealthy who reap the fruits of science and technology not the millions of poor. These facts are acknowledged openly every so often. For example, Monsanto's director of corporate communications told the *New York Times* on 25 October 1998, that the corporation should not have to take responsibility for the safety of its food products. "Monsanto should not have to vouchsafe the safety of biotech food," Phil Angell said. Cutting through the newspeak of the company's Pledge, he explained, "Our interest is in selling as much of it as possible."

Certainly, science and developing technology offer great possibilities for humanity. The problem lies in the responsible application and control of those technologies. This problem is at the heart of Rahul's play. He is expert at revealing the web of interests, competing, colliding, intermittent, colluding, opportunistic, overt, covert, conscious, and unconscious, that underscore arguments and proposals about wealth and economic development. His play is a powerful memorial and a tocsin. We would do well to listen, to remember, to remain vigilant, and to resist.

Guillermo Verdecchia
Toronto, 4 January 2004

After the gas.
photo by Prakash Hatvalne

Women survivors and Sambhavna Clinic Staff demanding Justice, Health Care,
Research, and Monitoring at the Indira Gandhi Hospital in Bhopal
on the occasion of International Women's Day.
photo by Terry Allan

After the gas.
photo by Prakash Hatvalne

Bhopal was first produced in Montreal by the Teesri Duniya Theatre at the Arts Interculturels, Montreal, in November 2001, with the following company:

Dr. Sonya Labonté	Rachell Glait
Izzat Bai	Micheline Dahlander
Devraj Sarthi	Shomee Chakrabartty
Minister Jaganlal Bhandari	Ivan Smith
Madiha Akram	Millie Tresierra
Pascale Sauvé	Nikija Malialin
Warren Anderson	Frank Fontaine
Story Teller	Shalini Lal
Chorus	Andrea Cochrane, Cortney Lohnes
	Young Choi, Dipti Gupta and Aliya Varma

Director	Jack Langedijk
Stage Manager	Kathryn Cleveland
Set Designer	Sheida Shojai
Light Design	Andrew Calamatas
Music	Scott Murray and Brian Vockeroth
Poster Designer	Tracy Martin

Bhopal was developed at the Cahoots Theatre Projects' Lift Off program; Teesri Duniya Theatre's intercultural play development program, Fireworks; and in the *PlayRites Colony 2000* at the Banff Centre for the Arts.

The author gratefully acknowledges the financial assistance from the Canada Council for the Arts, the Conseil des arts et des lettres du Québec, and Conseil des arts de Communauté Urbaine de Montréal.

Bhopal's Hindi translation, *Zahreeli Hawa*, was produced by Naya Theatre, India, in December 2002. The play toured six cities in India with the following company:

Dr. Sonya Labonté	Terry Allen
Izzat Bai	Aagesh Naag
Mr. Devraj Sarthi	Ram Chandra Singh
Minister Jaganlal Bhandari	Uday Ram Srivas
Madiha Akram	Choity Ghosh
Pascale Sauvé	Rajiv Yadava
Mr. Warren Anderson	David Francis

Chorus: Manoj Nayar, Yoshiko Vada, Rana Pratap Singh, Chandra Bhan Patel, Sheikh Arif, Sanyay Singh, Shyama Markaam, Nageen Tanvir, Tahira, Manharan Gandrarva, Chaitram Yadva, Amardas Manikpuri, Rama Shankar Rishi, Shivdayal Devdas, Dhannulal Sinha, Tajnoor, Onkardas Manikpuri, Abhisar Bose, Usman.

Translator/Director	Habib Tanvir
Stage Manager	Sheikh Arif
Costume	Monika Misra Tanvir
Set Design	Akhilesh Verma
Light Design	Dhannu Lal Sinha, Terry Allen
Music and Sound Effects	Nageen Tanvir
Publicity	Madan Soni
Harmonium	Rama Shankar Rishi
Tabla	Amardas Manikpuri
Dholak	Shivdayal Devdas
Majira	Manharan Gandrarva

Bhopal was produced by Cahoots Theatre Projects at the Theatre Centre, Toronto, in October/November 2003, with the following company:

Dr. Sonya Labonté	Brooke Johnson
Izzat Bai	Yashoda Ranganathan
Mr. Devraj Sarthi	Sugith Varughese
Minister Jaganlal Bhandari	Errol Sitahal
Madiha Akram	Imali Perera
Pascale Sauvé	Michael Miranda
Mr. Warren Anderson	Tom Butler

Director	Guillermo Verdecchia
Producer	Carlo Proto
Stage Manager	Sarah Dagleish
Set and Costume	Camellia Koo
Light Design/Production Manager	Michelle Ramsay
Sound Designer	Darren Copeland
Assistant Directors	Jovanni Sy and Oporajito Bhattacharjee
Assistant Stage Manager	Sherry Roher
Sound and Projection Operator	Jess Lyons

ACKNOWLEDGEMENTS

India's pre-eminent theatre artist Dr. Habib Tanvir, who conducted the very first workshop on the basis of a one-page synopsis I showed him during his visit to Montreal in 1997. His workshop taught me how to approach this play. In 2002 he translated *Bhopal* into Hindi as *Zahreeli Hawa*. The production of *Zahreeli Hawa* in Bhopal and other cities of India under Habib Tanvir's direction is a dream come true. Dr. Tanvir's association with this play is a matter of great honour for me.

Directors Tapan Bose and Suhasini Mulay, for their documentary "Bhopal: Beyond Genocide," which exposed me to the heart wrenching image of Zarina, a baby girl born after the accident.

Satinath Sarangi, Rashida Bie, and Champa Devi, most dedicated and tenacious activists, who introduced me to many of the survivors of Bhopal.

Dr. Daya Varma, my father, who started his research on survivors of Bhopal disaster within a month of the "accident." His untiring commitment to social causes continues to inspire me, and was the motivating force behind Dr. Sonya Labonté's character in *Bhopal*. Mrs. Krishna Varma, my mother, who is an example of resilience.

Paul Lefebvre, for his insightful dramaturgy and the translation of *Bhopal* into French.

Jack Langedijk, under whose direction *Bhopal* premiered in Montreal (2001). His contribution to the play went beyond that of a director and production dramaturge.

Guillermo Verdecchia, who sharpened my way of seeing this play. Dramaturges Ann Van Burik, Peter Hinton, and Brian Quirt for their valuable thoughts. My friend Sally Han who represents a turning point in my playwriting pursuit.

Kathryn Cleveland, who played a much bigger role in the premiere production in Montreal than what the title of Stage Manager suggests. Tracy Martin for designing an eye-catching poster for the play.

Ken McDonough, my friend, for editing my work with deep understanding of all I write. Ted Little, Laurel Sprengelmeyer, Anisa Cameron, and Carlo Proto, whose mere presence is a source of confidence. My wife, Dipti, and my daughter, Aliya—their role cannot be described in a one-line acknowledgement. My late step-brother Sanjay who was a committed environmentalist. Ila, Sonia, Sarah. Family. My brother Prem Saroj, all my nieces and nephews, who keep alive my attachment to India.

—RV

CHARACTERS

Dr. Sonya Labonté   A Canadian doctor and an activist who works with slum dwellers in Bhopal, India. She is the head of a Canadian non-governmental organisation (NGO) based in Bhopal India.

Izzat Bai   A young mother who lives in a Bhopal slum.

Devraj Sarthi   Head of the Indian subsidiary of an American multinational called Carbide International. He is an Indian national who was trained in the US and has returned to head Carbide International.

Jaganlal Bhandari   Chief Minister of the state in which city of Bhopal exists.

Madiha Akram   An employee at Carbide International. She is the personal assistant and lover of Mr. Sarthi.

Pascale Sauvé   Canadian Deputy Minister on a special assignment in India.

Warren Anderson   President and the supreme head of the parent Carbide International.

Chorus   Consisting of a singer, men, women, and children. (See note below.)

NOTE

About the Chorus: The chorus plays a wide range of roles, such as police officers, photographers, minister's aids, office workers, crowds, patients, and doctor's assistants. Except for the singer, I have restricted the chorus to non-speaking roles and have underwritten its action(s). The size of the chorus is flexible. The Montreal production had a five-member chorus, while the Indian production had more than twenty members.

SPECIAL CREDIT

The song "Ek Zahreeli Hawa" was written by Dr. Habib Tanvir especially for this play.

"Aise kihis bhagwan" is a tribal song from the state of Madhya Pradesh, which was given to me by Dr. Tanvir.

The play starts with a song. A dancer performs "Zahreeli Hawa" (poisoned gas) dance.

SINGER   Gaib say chalnay lagee jub
Ek Zahreeli Hawa
Dil kay phapholo say bhari
Kis kis kay nalo say bhari
Khamosh cheekho say bhari
Yeay kahan say utha rahi hai aisi dardili hawa
Gaib say chalnay lagee jub
Ek Zahreeli Hawa.

Ek mauzay lahoo aa rahee hai
Maut ki jaisi boo aa rahi hai
Kubooku suboosu aa rahi hai
Apni bayrangi maien bhi hai ek zara peeli hawa
Gaib say chalnay lagee jub ek Zahreeli Hawa

Scene I

Slum. IZZAT's hut. The police are taking SONYA away. Crowd follows them saying, "Police, police." DEVRAJ enters and stands at the mouth of IZZAT's hut. Slum dwellers start to converge at some distance, watching DEVRAJ. DEVRAJ knocks at IZZAT's door. IZZAT charges out of the hut.

IZZAT   Who is it? *(Shocked, seeing DEVRAJ, he turns to the crowd.)* Get the hell out of here, you no good rascals. What are you doing here? Uh??? *(crowd disperses, to DEVRAJ)* Oh forgive me *sahib*, I thought some police *wallah*... bloody father of law. Not a moment of peace from them.... You forgive me *sahib*?

DEVRAJ   Why do you seek forgiveness?

IZZAT	*Sahib*, I'm a poor woman, rotting in this slum. What do I know about law and order?
DEVRAJ	You don't need to worry.
IZZAT	How can I not worry, *sahib*? Who knows when one of them shows up, orders me to get lost, and flattens my hut...
DEVRAJ	That goat of yours... the one that died?
IZZAT	Yes, *sahib*. I'm not lying. My child lived on her milk. My own, my own chest, *sahib*, dried up long ago. I swear, *sahib*, my goat died. Do you want to check?
DEVRAJ	I believe you. *(gives her money)* Here, keep this.
IZZAT	*Maherbani sahib*, may God give you happiness, may you live a long life.
DEVRAJ	Let's go inside.
IZZAT	*Hai bhagawan.* My hut is uninhabitable for your comfort, *malik*. What can I offer you? My food may be too strong for your stomach. My water is undrinkable, for your standard. *(laughs)* Even I cannot digest my food, *malik*, how will you?
DEVRAJ	I need to talk to you. Let's go in.
	They step inside the hut.
IZZAT	*Sahib*, I'll run to the tea stall. A *tarak chai* or *masala*?
DEVRAJ	Don't bother.
IZZAT	I'm a poor woman, *sahib*, but I can't let you leave without sweetening your mouth, *sahib*.... Won't be long. Just from across the street...
DEVRAJ	Just stay. I don't have much time.
	A feeble sound of a baby is heard from a wooden basket. IZZAT picks up the basket.
DEVRAJ	What's that?
IZZAT	My Zarina! My little daughter.
DEVRAJ	*(looks inside)* Oh God! What has happened to her?

IZZAT	Don't let her fool you, *sahib*. She's a tough little monkey. God willing, she'll make me smile one day.
DEVRAJ	Did you bring her to a doctor?
IZZAT	Doctor Sonya Labonté, *sahib*, lady doctor Sonya!
DEVRAJ	Oh really! She's a good doctor...
IZZAT	But she doesn't know what Zarina has.
DEVRAJ	Well, does she know what you have?
IZZAT	Me, *sahib*?
DEVRAJ	You have poverty. Does the lady doctor Sonya know this?
IZZAT	What?
DEVRAJ	If you weren't poor, Zarina wouldn't be sick.
IZZAT	What are you saying, *sahib*?
DEVRAJ	Your little Zarina—she wasn't born sick, was she?
IZZAT	She, *sahib*? She was so sweet, her skin so smooth, so shiny, she looked like an angel at birth. Now she's always sick.
DEVRAJ	Of course. I don't know how you survive surrounded by filth.
IZZAT	Cleaning up filth costs money, *sahib*. Where's the money?
DEVRAJ	It's the filth that's the mother of all diseases. Among animals and among children! Someone told me there are other babies sick like Zarina. And they go to see this lady doctor, Dr. Sonya?
IZZAT	Yes, yes. I know them. I bring her patients.
DEVRAJ	Are they getting better?
IZZAT	Well... Veena, her baby... no! Budhiya... no, no, no, they don't get better.
DEVRAJ	Do you know Dr. Hans Weil?
IZZAT	No, *sahib*.

DEVRAJ	He lives behind the factory.
IZZAT	The yellow house?
DEVRAJ	That one. The yellow house! He is a tall man.
IZZAT	Pink skin. Thick cigar. I know who it is.
DEVRAJ	*(gives her a card)* Give him this. Take Zarina to him.
IZZAT	Yes.
DEVRAJ	And if anybody's animal dies, let me know. I will compensate.
IZZAT	Shanta's goat died yesterday and Kachari's pig passed away last week. You give me the money, *sahib*, and I will give it to them.
DEVRAJ	Thank you, but I prefer to give them the money myself.
IZZAT	*Theek hai, sahib.*
DEVRAJ	You give me the names of the mothers who visit this Doctor Sonya for their sick children.

> IZZAT picks up the basket. She holds DEVRAJ's card in her hand. She says the names of other women. DEVRAJ repeats the names after her.

IZZAT	Sure, *sahib*. Sure. Here. Veena, Budhiya, Kasturi, Shanta, Farida, Phoolmati, Babban, Meeta, Imarti, Roshni, Rani…
DEVRAJ	Not a word of that to Dr. Sonya. This is between you and me. Can you keep it that way?
IZZAT	My lips are sealed. I give you my word, *sahib*.

> DEVRAJ leaves. IZZAT says blessings for him.

Scene 2

> Detention cell. Chief Minister JAGANLAL talking to SONYA Labonté.

SONYA	For kidnapping?
JAGANLAL	Yes, for kidnapping.
SONYA	Have you gone completely insane?
JAGANLAL	Is that the way to talk to the chief minister?
SONYA	Who is charging me?
JAGANLAL	Doctor Labonté, I trusted you. I gave you a seat on the advisory board of one of my most important missions. I even granted you privileges reserved only for Indians. How can you stand there and tell me with a straight face that you were not abusing the privileges I granted you?
SONYA	Abusing? I have simply been carrying out the research you—
JAGANLAL	We both know you've been doing a great deal more than that. You have lost your perspective and completely overstepped the boundaries of your study.
SONYA	I'm just trying to help the women in your city. It's obvious what the problems are. Carbide is poisoning the—
JAGANLAL	Doctor, these are unfounded, uncorroborated allegations and—
SONYA	Have you read my research? Did you read any of the interim reports? Can anyone in your office read?
JAGANLAL	Your research will be impounded until we get to the bottom of this scam.
SONYA	You haven't even looked at it!
JAGANLAL	Whether or not I have read your material is not the issue, doctor. The issue is kidnapping. You have tried to smuggle two Indian citizens out of the country.
SONYA	I need to call my Embassy.
JAGANLAL	You *need* to?
SONYA	I'm a Canadian citizen.
JAGANLAL	Therefore what?

SONYA	I am a field physician with an UN-sanctioned NGO.
JAGANLAL	I've seen many such missionaries from the West.
SONYA	Mr. Minister, you can't do this to me!
JAGANLAL	Yes I can. Poor, hungry, destitute they may be, doctor, but the children of my country are sacred.

JAGANLAL exits.

Scene 3

Detention cell. Canadian diplomat Pascal SAUVÉ enters.

SAUVÉ	*(presenting his business card)* Pascal Sauvé, Government of Canada.
SONYA	They won't tell me who is charging me.
SAUVÉ	It's my duty to help troubled Canadians abroad.
SONYA	They're trying to bury my research.
SAUVÉ	Well, then let's get you out of here.
SONYA	These charges are completely trumped up. The minister or somebody close to him doesn't like the work I'm doing and they've invented this. My research points to some very serious problems and they think they can scare me and I'll just stop.
SAUVÉ	Doctor, all I want to do is get you back home safely.
SONYA	I don't want to go home. I want to get out of here, clear my name, and do my work.
SAUVÉ	*(pulls out some papers from her suitcase)* Well, first we need to work through some problems before we can say what will happen.
SONYA	You believe me, don't you?
SAUVÉ	*(showing her a document)* This, I believe, is yours.

SONYA	What's that?
SAUVÉ	A requisition for two plane tickets.
SONYA	Okay.
SAUVÉ	*(pulls out a visa document)* And a visa application for Izzat.
SONYA	Isn't that supposed to be confidential?
SAUVÉ	What? The application or the fact that you signed for her?
SONYA	Nothing wrong with that! She gave me the right to—
SAUVÉ	Nothing to worry about then. *(pointing at the photograph on the visa document)* So you know this woman?
SONYA	Izzat. Yes.
SAUVÉ	What is your relationship with her?
SONYA	She's one of my study subjects.
SAUVÉ	What did you tell her, Dr. Labonté?
SONYA	About what?
SAUVÉ	I need to know what you told her.
SONYA	*(in frustration)* I told her I was doing a study on women's health. That I would be collecting data pertaining to women's reproductive health in the slum. I would be examining women and their babies.
SAUVÉ	And did you promise her treatment if she came to Canada?
	Flashback: SONYA's clinic. IZZAT lying on the floor. SONYA is examining IZZAT's stomach and vaginal area. Member(s) of the CHORUS have become SONYA's assistant(s). Zarina's basket sits nearby.
IZZAT	My stomach burns, feels hot inside.
SONYA	Are you menstruating normally?
IZZAT	I bleed a lot.

SONYA	Thick and dry?
IZZAT	A lot of mucky blood.
SONYA	Open your legs.
IZZAT	No, *doctorni sahiba*, no, my… this thing is a mess.
SONYA	I will have to send you to Dr. Bhalerao.
IZZAT	I don't need this thing anymore. Zarina's father is dead.
SONYA	That's okay. You may sit up. Dr. Bhalerao must see this.

IZZAT gets up, picks up Zarina's basket.

IZZAT	Don't worry about me, *doctorni sahiba*, you help Zarina.

SONYA starts examining Zarina.

SONYA	And her lungs are… weak, Izzat. Her breathing? It's difficult, hard for her. I don't know, can't tell right now, if there's actual tissue damage to the lungs but…
IZZAT	Why, doctor?
SONYA	Well, again it's difficult to say exactly, Izzat. There are any number of factors involved, many reasons. But given your own condition, the discharge, the cervical erosion—and it's consistent with what I'm seeing in a lot of the other women—I think there's a contaminant, poisons, in your body that got into Zarina's body, and—
IZZAT	You help Zarina?
SONYA	Izzat, there's not much I can do here. Her arm is not going to grow. Her breathing…. Give her clean water, Izzat, clean milk. Keep her close, warm, hold her. We can keep her comfortable. I can't promise—

IZZAT scoops Zarina up from the basket and moves away.

IZZAT	No. The company doctor says Zarina—
SONYA	What? Did you go to the company doctor? Hans Weil? Did you? Dr. Hans Weil?

IZZAT	Uh?
SONYA	Big hair, moustache?
IZZAT	No.
SONYA	Good.
IZZAT	He came to see me.
SONYA	Give me a straight answer, Izzat.
IZZAT	Sarthi *sahib* came by my hut. He said he wants to help me.
SONYA	Mr. Devraj Sarthi… the president of Carbide… he came to your hut?
IZZAT	To help me.
SONYA	Money?
IZZAT	God bless his soul.
SONYA	Oh yes, God bless his soul, he'll help you all right. He's the one making the poison.
IZZAT	How do you talk?
SONYA	You are forbidden to see another doctor. You come to me if there's a problem, Izzat. Go and wash up now.
IZZAT	I'm sorry.
SONYA	Just go.
	IZZAT goes to wash her feet. SONYA follows IZZAT and shows her some photographs.
SONYA	Where are these women?
IZZAT	Hasina? Kasturi??
SONYA	And why haven't they come to see me?
IZZAT	They are not seeing anybody.
SONYA	But I want to see them. I need to examine their babies.
IZZAT	Women are not talking.
SONYA	Why?

IZZAT   That's what we do—we don't talk when we lose
           someone in the family.

SONYA   So the babies are dead? Their babies are dead? *(IZZAT
           nods "yes.")* Where are the bodies? When did they die?
           Why didn't you come and get me? They are crucial to
           my study.

IZZAT   You never told me.

SONYA   Listen to me carefully, Izzat. What I'm doing is good
           for you. Understand? What I am doing for you is
           something nobody else would do. And it's the best
           thing for Zarina. Do you understand? That's what we
           talked about and you signed it.

IZZAT   Thumbprint?

SONYA   Right, and you didn't tell anyone did you?

IZZAT   Plan to go to Canada? Zarina and me? Thumbprint.
           No.

SONYA   Good.

           *SONYA returns to her charts and files, makes notes.
           Flashback ends.*

SAUVÉ   Dr. Labonté we didn't give you a grant to fly Izzat to
           Canada, did we?

SONYA   I did what's best for my patient.

SAUVÉ   She's not your patient. She is a study subject.

SONYA   She is my patient. These women, they don't have
           doctors. They don't have—

SAUVÉ   What about this company doctor?

SONYA   That doctor is ex-Pentagon.

SAUVÉ   Well, doctor, we fund non-governmental organisations
           to promote Canadian values abroad not to—

SONYA   You want me to ignore what is happening to these
           women? Is that a Canadian value? Carbide is violating
           more than one of India's laws! The Obnoxious

	Industry Law says companies like Carbide have to be at least fifteen miles from populous areas.
SAUVÉ	There are so many laws, it is impossible not to break a few. But that's a matter for the Indian officials. Their laws are their business.
SONYA	I can show you my research—or I could if I knew where it was—Carbide is draining toxic waste into the lake, the pond. The children *play* in that water… people bathe in it and fall sick of diseases unknown to medical science.
SAUVÉ	Unknown to medical science?
SONYA	If you want to see a human baby that is not necessarily a human baby, go to the slum.
SAUVÉ	Dr. Labonté, I advise you to sign this.
SONYA	I'm not signing anything.
SAUVÉ	You are in serious trouble, doctor. I can get you out of here and back to Canada if you sign this.
SONYA	So they can say I'm guilty? I'm not quitting. These women need me.
SAUVÉ	Well, I leave you to weigh your options.

SAUVÉ exits.

Scene 4

Waiting area of DEVRAJ's office. SAUVÉ enters.

SAUVÉ	I'd like to speak to Sarthi Devraj.
MADIHA	Devraj Sarthi. I'm sorry, but he's not here.
SAUVÉ	When will he be in?
MADIHA	Tomorrow morning at 8am!
SAUVÉ	Then I shall come back tomorrow morning.

MADIHA	Maybe I can help you.
SAUVÉ	*(starting to leave)* No, thank you, I need to talk to him directly.
MADIHA	I am his executive assistant you know. I sometimes know more about what goes on here than he does. *(SAUVÉ stops.)* So, what trouble is he in?
SAUVÉ	Do you know a Doctor Sonya Labonté?
MADIHA	Yes.
SAUVÉ	Have you ever spoken to her?
MADIHA	Yes, many times. That woman keeps trying to destroy this company.
SAUVÉ	Pardon me?
MADIHA	She accuses us of the most outrageous things.
SAUVÉ	Such as?
MADIHA	All that Mr. Sarthi does is help these people.

> *Flashback: DEVRAJ's office. IZZAT enters with her basket. MADIHA notices her with annoyance.*

IZZAT	*Memsahib, memsahib, memsahib.*
MADIHA	Told you, don't call me *memsahib.*
IZZAT	I call *sahib... sahib* so I should call *memsahib... memsahib.*
MADIHA	Is it a goat? What is it this time? A dog? A rat? We're not paying for any more of your dead animals.
IZZAT	*Sahib* said...
MADIHA	*Chalo Raasta Napo. (Beat. Her eyes on the basket, MADIHA walks towards IZZAT.)* Let me see...
IZZAT	No! For *sahib*!
MADIHA	You probably kill them yourself just to get the money. You can dodge him but I'm not a fool.

> *DEVRAJ enters.*

Oh, Mr. Sarthi... Mr. Sarthi.

IZZAT	*(to DEVRAJ)* I begged the *chowkidar, sahib,* because I wanted to show it to you right in your hand.
DEVRAJ	All right, show me what?
MADIHA	Another dead animal.
DEVRAJ	Miss Akram.
IZZAT	*(to DEVRAJ)* Look, look inside—
MADIHA	Which, I'm sure is not hers—
IZZAT	Getting worse, *sahib.* See one more time, please, *sahib*—
MADIHA	She probably picked it up from the street—
DEVRAJ	Wait, Miss Akram—
MADIHA	Don't pay her a *dhela.*
IZZAT	Oh, please… please… look.
MADIHA	She says the company kills their animals. They are doing it themselves.
IZZAT	*(to MADIHA)* No, no. You look.
	MADIHA pulls away the rag covering the basket and is visibly shocked at what she sees inside. We hear ZARINA's cry. IZZAT grabs the basket and runs to a corner. A hush sets in.
DEVRAJ	*(to MADIHA)* This is her baby. *(to IZZAT)* What do you want me to do? Didn't you bring her to Hans? Dr. Hans Weil?
IZZAT	I did. But she's getting worse.
DEVRAJ	He will treat her. I am not a doctor. *(puts two one-hundred rupee notes in her palm)*
	Flashback ends.
MADIHA	Mr. Sarthi goes out of his way to help these people and she tries—
SAUVÉ	Dr. Labonté?
MADIHA	Yes. She tries to twist it into something awful.

SAUVÉ   Does she?

MADIHA   Mr. Sarthi makes the company doctor available to these women and Labonté comes here, right into the office, and accuses the company doctor of stealing her patients, taking mothers and their babies from her clinic. Those women come here for money; they are very skilled beggars. It makes no sense. And she claims Carbide Thunder is poisonous. That the company is poisoning these people in their shacks around the factory. As if the company would do such a thing. We manufacture pesticides, you know. These chemicals, they improve the lives of everyone. If you could hear Devraj talk about how Carbide Thunder will change everyone's life, you'd soon see that that woman has malice in her heart.

SAUVÉ   I see.

MADIHA   I see you're from Canada?

SAUVÉ   Yes.

MADIHA   Take her back, and keep her there. We have enough problems.

SAUVÉ   Thank you for your time.

           SAUVÉ departs.

Scene 5

           A party hosted by JAGANLAL. Festive mood. CHORUS members act as guests. DEVRAJ and MADIHA enter. JAGANLAL greets them with great enthusiasm.

JAGANLAL   Ladies and gentlemen, Mr. Devraj Sarthi!

DEVRAJ   Thank you, Mr. Minister. What have I done to deserve such an honour?

JAGANLAL	I want to shake your hand, Mr. Sarthi. You're a great NRI.
DEVRAJ	NRI?
MADIHA	Non-resident Indian.
JAGANLAL	Not really Indian! Har, har, har... and *aadab* to you Madam...?
MADIHA	*(shaking hands with JAGANLAL)* Madiha Akram, Mr. Minister.
JAGANLAL	How so very wonderful to see women acting as equals. You have no idea how much I have anticipated this dinner tonight. Are you prepared to make a speech?
DEVRAJ	Speech?
JAGANLAL	A little after-dinner speech!
MADIHA	Of course, do it!
DEVRAJ	On the People's Progress Zone?
JAGANLAL	How must I introduce you? People say you're blinded by your feelings for the poor.
MADIHA	No doubt about that.
JAGANLAL	And you're an animal lover.
MADIHA	In a strange sort of way...
JAGANLAL	How so? How must I point that out?
MADIHA	He created the Animal Charity Fund.
JAGANLAL	I've heard great things about that.
DEVRAJ	The Animal Charity Fund is a public service. Sometimes, especially now due to this drought, animals die and people leave the dead animals on the streets.
MADIHA	And when they start to rot they contaminate the drinking water.
DEVRAJ	Thank you, Miss Akram. *(turns to JAGANLAL)* Yes, in order to prevent disease from spreading, we encourage the people to bring the dead animals to Carbide International and we compensate them. That helps

them, and certainly doesn't hurt our company image. That's what I call the Animal Charity Fund.

JAGANLAL   Animal Charity Fund, compensation…. Brilliant! Just brilliant.

MADIHA   Charity.

JAGANLAL   Excellent. Until yesterday, America had sent India its hippies, druggies, and devotees. In you, Mr. Sarthi, I see a new man. An exceptional NRI who went to America to learn, design, and build, and then returned to heal his home country.

             Flashback: DEVRAJ being interviewed by ANDERSON for the post of CEO of the Indian branch of Carbide International.

ANDERSON   I know that, but what city in India?

DEVRAJ   From Lucknow, sir.

ANDERSON   And you've been with the company for eight years?

DEVRAJ   Yes.

ANDERSON   Now you want to go back home?

DEVRAJ   It's just the sort of challenge that I'm looking for. I was friends with the son of my family's maidservant when I was young. I used to give him half of my lunch at school. When we grew up, I got a business degree and he ended up pulling a rickshaw. It was winter when I left for the US and he came to see me off at the airport. I gave him my coat. As I walked through the gate I saw my mother, superior as always, walk up to him with a dirty look on her face and I'm sure an insulting taunt on her tongue. Right then and there, I swore to myself that I'd come back.

             Beat.

ANDERSON   What are your thoughts on DDT?

DEVRAJ   In my opinion, sir, Carbide Thunder will replace DDT.

ANDERSON   You'd like to be known as the pest that killed DDT.

DEVRAJ   Because DDT has been found in bird populations.

ANDERSON	Aw, poor birds. *(testing him)* What about the millions it has saved from malaria?
DEVRAJ	But it's a carcinogen. I believe, sir, that Carbide Thunder is a superior product. Not only does it spare the bird population, it's also non-carcinogenic.
ANDERSON	I'm sure you're aware there are scientific studies that suggest there are other deleterious side effects.
DEVRAJ	I would put my faith in scientific studies if they truly prove the point they claim to be proving. But, we know, one study proves a product is a health hazard, another proves the contrary. So I plan to prove something that's beyond any doubt, and that is that Carbide Thunder is safer than DDT, cheaper to produce than DDT, and sure to tilt India's trade potential.
ANDERSON	And what about Carbide International, Mr. Sarthi? We are, you know, looking to improve our performance.
DEVRAJ	Sir, India offers us a competitive advantage in many ways.
ANDERSON	I have to tell you that India is looking more and more marginal to us, Mr Sarthi. We need someone who will cut costs and improve productivity.
DEVRAJ	Sir, our offshore operations generate fourteen percent of revenue but account for twenty-three percent of our profits. I am confident that I can find ways to make our India operation more efficient and productive. Carbide Thunder is the key, sir.
ANDERSON	You think so?
DEVRAJ	I'm sure of it, sir.
ANDERSON	I like that, son. The hero◌ have a vision, and are wi
DEVRAJ	If something can keep h it will more than make ᵢ Anderson, given the ch Thunder will touch ma

Flashback ends. DEVRAJ resumes his conversation with JAGANLAL.

JAGANLAL   India needs more men like you.

DEVRAJ   India deserves a shot in the arm.

JAGANLAL   Shot?

DEVRAJ   Boost its production capacity.

JAGANLAL   All poor countries deserve a shot in the arm.

DEVRAJ   India is not poor, sir, it's simply forgotten.

JAGANLAL   It's about time somebody said that.

DEVRAJ   If we want the world to respect us, India's output must be increased tenfold.

JAGANLAL   Quite right!

DEVRAJ   Granted your approval, I am prepared to increase our production tenfold.

JAGANLAL   And reduce your costs, I believe?

DEVRAJ   We've discussed the People's Progress Zone. It's like a country within a country.

JAGANLAL   *Achha.*

DEVRAJ   Free of bureaucratic barriers, an area of deregulation.

JAGANLAL   Okay.

DEVRAJ   Such incentives are needed to increase the country's industrial base, to generate wealth, and, yes, to support our efforts to produce profitable chemicals.

JAGANLAL   Pesticides, you mean?

DEVRAJ   As you may have seen in my submission, pesticides have recorded a quarter century of sustained growth. Under the People's Progress Zone plan, we can manufacture upwards of five to ten thousand tons of Carbide Thunder a year. But the quantity is not the important thing.

      It's the quality. Pesticides are peaceful. They are not like chemicals of war.

JAGANLAL	Right, they just war against pests.
MADIHA	Of course. The pests will not be gi... poor people's food and leave them... let me tell you one more thing, Mr... an average Indian today, like myself, like yourself, we live better than the maharajas—because of the kind of chemicals Carbide produces.
JAGANLAL	Yes, yes. Although, Carbide Thunder is used for cotton, not for peoples' food.
DEVRAJ	But pesticides generally improve—
JAGANLAL	Of course. But I'm concerned. I've heard a rumour that Dr. Bhalerao is planning judicial action to stop the People's Progress Zone and Dr. Labonté's study is being cited as a proof of—
MADIHA	That woman? She thinks Carbide Thunder is poisoning everyone. That woman just won't stop.
DEVRAJ	Miss Akram. *(to JAGANLAL)* They are worried someone might drink Carbide Thunder.
JAGANLAL	Drink it?
DEVRAJ	As if someone would drink pesticide. But even if Carbide Thunder got into your body…
JAGANLAL	My body?
DEVRAJ	…it would only cause coughing, sneezing, and minor itching. Then it would be hydrolyzed.
JAGANLAL	*(sighs)* Aaah… *(thinks)* What?
DEVRAJ	Our company doctor, Hans Weil, confirms that it will roll out via the eyes.
JAGANLAL	Like tears?
DEVRAJ	Like tears!
JAGANLAL	Aaah! …Is your Bhopal plant identical to the one in the US?
DEVRAJ	Of course!

GANLAL	And Carbide Thunder will roll out of American eyes like ours, in the form of tears?

DEVRAJ nods affirmatively.

Any proof?

MADIHA	Mr. Minister, let us invite these people to this dinner and feed them Carbide Thunder.
DEVRAJ	Miss Akram?
JAGANLAL	What?
MADIHA	Yes! To prove that it will roll out of their eyes.
JAGANLAL	Brilliant.
DEVRAJ	Of course we wouldn't need to do that.

Transition to the after-dinner speech.

Mr. Minister, on the way to your office, I passed through the slum. It was filled with open garbage, the heat was suffocating, and the stench of human excrement was unbearable. I stumbled over drunken men, saw babies hanging from their mothers' breasts, and encountered stubborn seven- and eight-year-old boys with faces that said that if I didn't give them some change, they'd die of hunger. I met a woman, a poor woman, who told me that her first child died of worms that crawled out of its body. Why? How did this happen? There are those who will blame industrial development. Chemicals like our Carbide Thunder. Obviously, that is not the case; we always think of safety first. But environmental safeguards are irrelevant if we don't attack poverty first, for it is the poverty that is our greatest environmental hazard. Yes, my efforts aren't reaching the people yet. But with my plan in place, the benefits will trickle all the way down to the poorest of the poor. That's why we need the People's Progress Zone.

Applause.

JAGANLAL	That storm of applause is for you.
MADIHA	That was wonderful.

DEVRAJ	Really?
MADIHA	Yes.
JAGANLAL	Mr. Sarthi, that was a very moving speech. People in this room, my staff and dignitaries, froze as you talked, and we now know we want to hear more from you. Yes, you must boost production. *(announcing)* Ladies and gentlemen, the first gift of the People's Progress Zone. *(eyes set on DEVRAJ)* Carbide will build seven hundred new houses!
DEVRAJ	Seven hundred new houses?
JAGANLAL	But of course! When you expand the Carbide complex...
DEVRAJ	But I don't remember promising seven hundred new houses...

> *Before DEVRAJ can answer, JAGANLAL walks up to him, stands face to face with him, and clasps both his hands in a traditional namastay.*

JAGANLAL	That, Mr. Sarthi, must be the necessary gift of Carbide to my people.

> *JAGANLAL departs to loud applause from the CHORUS.*

DEVRAJ	Well... in that case, I must name it Jaganlal Colony.

> *More applause from the dispersing crowd.*

Scene 6

> *Next day. MADIHA in DEVRAJ's office. DEVRAJ enters and grabs her in his arms. She frees herself and steps away from him.*

MADIHA	Did you see the look in people's eyes?
DEVRAJ	What people?

MADIHA	At the party!
DEVRAJ	People looked victorious seeing the look on my face.
MADIHA	What?
DEVRAJ	When Jaganlal volunteered me to build seven hundred new houses.
MADIHA	I'm not talking about that look.
DEVRAJ	What look are you talking about then?
MADIHA	The look that says, "Look at that slut."
DEVRAJ	Darling, don't start that one.
MADIHA	You know what people think about me?
DEVRAJ	Please!
MADIHA	I blackened my name for you.
DEVRAJ	We have talked about it many times.
MADIHA	So what are you going to do about it?
DEVRAJ	I have something for you. *(gives her a gift)* Open it.
	Before she can open the gift, he opens it for her.
MADIHA	Devraj, what is this?
	He puts a locket around her neck.
DEVRAJ	With this, I make you a promise.
MADIHA	Yes?
DEVRAJ	I'll be yours, I promise, but I can't handle marriage.
MADIHA	Then what's the promise?
DEVRAJ	Marriage like a sacred duty or marriage like a burden? What mother wants for me? The way she married? It's a no, not for me. We don't need to be married to be together, do we?
	They embrace. Sound effects take us to the next scene.

Scene 7

> One week later. JAGANLAL visits the slum with his
> entourage. Reporters, cameramen, the members of
> the CHORUS as citizens and slum dwellers follow
> him.

JAGANLAL No, no, no. Don't take a photo yet. Over here!

> Slum dwellers begin to assemble. JAGANLAL notices
> IZZAT in the crowd.

You, *Bai*! *(calling)* Would you? Yes, yes, please—come
here... stand here... don't move. *(in part to himself and
in part to the media)* When I see a woman like you, *bai*,
a voice inside me says, "Go hug her. Pick her child up
in your arms, and give her your shawl."

> Puts his shawl over her shoulders.

IZZAT May God give you long life, *mantri ji*.

JAGANLAL Okay. Now. Smile. *(She smiles.)* No, no, not like that,
like this. *(He models a smile and she imitates him.)* Like
that, okay. *(Cameras start flashing.)* I'm sick of having
my photograph taken. If I catch any one of these
photographers, I will shoot to kill...

> IZZAT steps out of the photo-shoot.

IZZAT Me too, *mantri ji*.

JAGANLAL I feel very close to you, *bai*, so close that I want to
drink from your glass and eat from your plate.

IZZAT Honour is all mine, *mantri ji*, but I don't have much on
my plate.

JAGANLAL Where is your hut, *bai*?

IZZAT Do you see this *pagdandi*?

JAGANLAL I'm standing on it.

IZZAT This *pagdandi* snakes through garbage, shit, and dead
animals.

JAGANLAL Bad, very bad...

IZZAT	All the way to the pond. Do you see the pond?
JAGANLAL	*Haan, haan…*
IZZAT	From the pond one *pagdandi* goes this way—to the lake—and the other goes that way—to the company. There, my hut is there.
JAGANLAL	I have decided to demolish it.
IZZAT	Oh, no… oh no, please… I beg *mantri ji*… I'm a poor woman…
JAGANLAL	But I am going to do something about it.
IZZAT	*Mantri ji*, please, my husband lost everything to the bottle. And I ended up here. I made my hut behind the railway. The *chowkidar*… "*hut haramzadi*"…
JAGANLAL	Your hut—
IZZAT	Then, I made a home between the fences and the *mandir* and the *pundit ji* chased me, "*Chal bhag. Bhagwan kay ghar say.*" Then I go… under bridge… on sidewalk… by the gutter… "*bhaag, hatt bhaag.*"
JAGANLAL	Now *bai*, your new house—
IZZAT	Finally I made this shack… my home… in shadow of *sahib's* company…
JAGANLAL	But having your home here doesn't make you legal.
IZZAT	In front of all these people… *mantri ji*, these people are my witness… I don't know rules and regulations. In front of all these people, *mantri ji*, I say I will not leave my hut even if you kill me. In the name of all these people, *mantri ji*, be merciful. *(showing Zarina's basket)* I have a sick baby.
JAGANLAL	I'm sorry, this hut of yours will be replaced with a house!
IZZAT	What will happen to me, *mantri ji*?
JAGANLAL	You, *bai*… you will live in that house.
IZZAT	What?
JAGANLAL	Your hearing is fine, *bai*. You will own the house.

IZZAT	Me? House? Mine? But… but…
JAGANLAL	But what, *bai*?
IZZAT	It feels like a promise.
JAGANLAL	And didn't I promise a water tap in the *basti* last year?
IZZAT	We were hoping for some water from it this year.
JAGANLAL	Such life—such life here! You are the ray of hope. *(to media, crowd)* This *bai* is right. I hereby announce— and you media people note me and quote me— through the authority vested in me as the chief minister and the head of the new Super Ministry for Trade Liberalization, I declare that Bhopal Lake, the connecting bridge and the railway station—all this area surrounding Carbide International—to be known as the People's Progress Zone, a new, independent governing zone which will also be known as the PPZ.
IZZAT	PeePeeZeee…
JAGANLAL	The PPZ will be a model site. A country within a country with distinct rules! To help us help our people. To catch up on decades of underdevelopment! As of today, all inhabitants of the Peoples Progress Zone will own the piece of land on which their illegal huts sit. *Bai*—
IZZAT	May God give you longest life, *mantri ji*, I'll have a real home. God be merciful, this means a ration card and right to vote!
JAGANLAL	This is not for your vote *bai*. This is for real.
IZZAT	Oh?
JAGANLAL	You are the first citizen of the People's Progress Zone. Yes. And here is a sample of what your home will look like.

> *He distributes pictures of model homes to the slum dwellers.*

This is for you. This, *maa ji*, this is for you.

> *IZZAT calls other slum dwellers. They are happy, comparing photographs of their prospective homes.*

IZZAT   I live in this, in the paper. Imrati. Babu. Come here. Look, my home… window and indoor *snadas*… no more shutting the bowel from sunrise to sunset, no, noo… no more going behind the bush to do the business. And hey, look, a water tap.

Scene 8

> *One week later. Sauvé, who has just returned from the Canadian High Commission in New Delhi, visits JAGANLAL. SAUVÉ opens a document.*

SAUVÉ   Mr. Minister, may I be frank with you?

JAGANLAL   Please.

SAUVÉ   Either you free Doctor Labonté or lose India's Preferred Trading status.

JAGANLAL   One woman is more important than two countries?

> *SAUVÉ gives him a document.*

SAUVÉ   As you know, our next bilateral trade summit is in Montreal.

JAGANLAL   I will say a line or two in French in my opening speech.

SAUVÉ   The problem is, sir, that Labonté is scheduled to speak at a parallel conference taking place next door to our trade talks.

JAGANLAL   Not if she's in my custody. I won't have anyone distracting attention from my presentation.

SAUVÉ   That's exactly what will happen if you keep her in jail. Protesters will throw themselves against the fences and throw tear gas at a time when the eyes of the world are set on our Prime Minister.

JAGANLAL	You want me to drop the charges against this doctor so your Prime Minister will have one less headache?
SAUVÉ	Quite frankly, sir, it is a trade headache.
JAGANLAL	I don't accept that.
SAUVÉ	Sir, it has taken years to prepare Canada for your trade mission. Our countries are setting an example in bilateral trade that will make the world envious. But when you and your trade delegation arrive in Canada, the media won't leave us alone, sir. Labonté is Canadian, after all, and her arrest is… dramatic. It will make things very difficult for us. Canada will be embarrassed and will have a hard time ratifying contracts and treaties signed with you.
JAGANLAL	Free a women who kidnaps mothers and children to bad-mouth my country abroad?
SAUVÉ	Sir, sooner or later the world will come to know that she wasn't kidnapping. She was just trying to bring a mother and her sick child to a conference in Canada. Forgive me for saying this—people would not only see her as a victim, but would also say that you caved in to Carbide.
JAGANLAL	That's nonsense.
SAUVÉ	Sir, I'm pleading for the success of our trade talks. If you don't sign her release, Carbide International will applaud you but Canadian trade and aid to India will not increase.
JAGANLAL	I do not appreciate blackmail from a trade partner.
SAUVÉ	Our government and transnationals don't want to have to answer embarrassing questions about the way a high-profile Canadian is treated by a trade partner. They'll be quite happy to invest in one of the seventy-five countries around the world whose GDP is less than their corporation's profit. You asked me to be frank, I'm being frank.

SAUVÉ retrieves the document and moves as if to leave.

JAGANLAL	What does the document say?
SAUVÉ	It contains an apology: she relinquishes all rights to her research, and accepts a lifetime ban from working in India.
JAGANLAL	Bring her in.
	SONYA enters (is "brought in").
JAGANLAL	Is this your first visit to India?
SONYA	First to a jail.
JAGANLAL	The children of my country are not your props.
SONYA	Nor should they be casualties of Carbide—
JAGANLAL	You have been here barely long enough to see a few malnourished kids and—
SONYA	And a lot of poisoned kids.
JAGANLAL	And you're in the habit of not seeing the millions of healthy kids.
SONYA	There aren't any healthy kids in the slums.
SAUVÉ	Well, madam doctor, Mr. Minister, I brought you both here—
JAGANLAL	I want to let this lady know something. *(to SONYA)* Sit down. *(She sits.)* Maybe your research is accurate, maybe our housing project is a bad idea. Maybe the People's Progress Zone is a big mistake. Maybe the children of Bhopal are really unlike any human beings you have ever seen before. But I don't need a foreigner to exhibit a sick child of my country in a foreign land. Doctor, we can look after our sick. I resent white people showing me what's best for my people. Anyway, I didn't mean to say that. My last comment wasn't intentional.
SAUVÉ	We understand.
JAGANLAL	Mr. Sauvé has persuaded me to drop the charges against you.
SAUVÉ	You will sign this apology.

SONYA	Apology? For what?
SAUVÉ	That's the deal.
SONYA	Apologise?
SAUVÉ	And accept a lifetime ban.
SONYA	Are you out of your mind? I'll stay here.

SAUVÉ takes SONYA a few steps away.

SAUVÉ	Excuse me, Mr. Minister. Use your head, doctor.
SONYA	Who would believe that bringing a mother and her sick child to Canada is kidnapping?
SAUVÉ	I don't think you live in the real world.
SONYA	Izzat wanted to go. She knew that it was the best thing for her and Zarina.

SAUVÉ gives SONYA an affidavit.

SAUVÉ	This is in English, doctor! The woman didn't know what she was putting her thumbprint on!
SONYA	Bring her here and she will tell you.
SAUVÉ	She's the one who charged you.
SONYA	She did?

SAUVÉ pulls SONYA aside.

SAUVÉ	Look Labonté, if you sign now, you can go somewhere else and carry on your research. Maybe—maybe you can find a way to get back to India and resume your work. On the other hand, if you want to be "principled," well, maybe the CBC will do a documentary on you, or environmentalists will circulate an on-line petition for your release, but you won't see daylight for fifteen years. Which one do you want?

> *SAUVÉ holds up a pen to SONYA, who is silent. He walks towards JAGANLAL. SONYA follows. SAUVÉ gestures both to sign the deal.*

SONYA	I'll sign this, but it won't shut me up. I'll sign this, but it won't silence me.
SAUVÉ	Mr. Minister.

> *JAGANLAL signs, then SAUVÉ puts his own
> signature. JAGANLAL extends his hand to shake
> SAUVÉ's, but SAUVÉ in return clasps his hands
> in traditional namastay.*

> *Marché conclu. (to SONYA)* This prohibits you from
> Carbide International and the PPZ. Your plane leaves
> December 3rd, 1984, at 0100 hours from Bhopal
> International Airport.

JAGANLAL	A government car will take you to the airport. My people will make sure you catch your plane with no inconvenience.
SAUVÉ	Congratulations, you are allowed to return to Canada.

> *SONYA angrily crushes the deal. Exits.*

Scene 9

> *Outside IZZAT's hut. SONYA enters. Zarina's basket
> is absent.*

SONYA	Izzat. How could you be so stupid?
IZZAT	*Mafi, doctorni sahiba!*
SONYA	How much did they pay you? What did you think would happen, eh?
IZZAT	Okay, okay, *doctorni sahiba*, don't shout.
SONYA	Do you know what they've done?
IZZAT	I'm sorry, *doctorni sahiba*...
SONYA	You're sorry!! They stole my research. I have nothing to present at the conference. All my surveys, blood, urine

samples—everything—is destroyed. Th
bulldozed, and I'll be put on a plane tom

IZZAT	You will go?
SONYA	Yes! Zarina would have received the best treatment of her life. Now she will get nothing…. Where is Zarina?
IZZAT	She's sleeping.
SONYA	She's alone? I want to see her.
IZZAT	No! My man is back.
SONYA	Your man is dead!
IZZAT	Leave me alone, *doctorni sahiba*!
SONYA	Where is she?
IZZAT	She was my baby, my little angel. I don't want anyone to see her. She was my baby.
SONYA	She's dead? *(long pause)* Where is her body? They bought her body, didn't they? Money? How much? You sold your baby.
IZZAT	No.
SONYA	Like Hasina.
IZZAT	No.
SONYA	Like Kastoori.
IZZAT	No.
SONYA	You sold your own child.
IZZAT	*(breaking into tears)* Satan invaded my heart. Satan took money for Zarina. Devil in me did that. Devil lived in my stomach. I don't need this money. *(pulls out a few rupees from her blouse and throws them towards SONYA)* Throw this away into the gutter, I don't need it.
SONYA	The Devil lives in the company's poison… you fool.
IZZAT	Me, fool?

SONYA	The company killed Zarina and gave you some cash for her dead body and you came home thinking that the company did you an act of charity.
IZZAT	You don't know how I survive, *doctorni sahiba*. Why do you harass me?
SONYA	If money is all you wanted, this is nothing compared to what I could have got for you. You fool.
IZZAT	You? You cannot fool me! No clinic, no research, no treating, nothing, just a big mouth. What you want, huh? You want to take my daughter to a foreign country to show her. What will that say about my daughter? Huh? What will people say? What kind of mother is she, showing her daughter to everyone—her twisted hands, her heaving chest, her melting skin, shame on the mother who did that to her child. And who wants to look at my Zarina? How dare you? My daughter is in peace. I have peace. Why do you come between us? Please, *doctorni sahib*, please, be merciful to me, be merciful to my daughter, let my daughter have peace.

Scene 10

DEVRAJ's office. DEVRAJ enters. SONYA storms into the office.

SONYA	What are you doing? What the hell are you doing?
DEVRAJ	You're not supposed to be here, doctor.
SONYA	Stop it, damn it, stop killing everything that lives around this factory.
DEVRAJ	*Chowkidar!*
SONYA	Your Peoples' Progress Zone, your cover-up.
DEVRAJ	Get on your plane, white woman.
SONYA	Bloody coconut.

MADIHA	This woman does not stop.
SONYA	*(turning to MADIHA)* Do you know what his company has been doing? *(to DEVRAJ)* Does she know your company doctor paid my patients for their babies?
DEVRAJ	Out! Out of here!
SONYA	Twenty-seven dead babies—
MADIHA	What is she talking about?
DEVRAJ	Where the hell is security?
SONYA	Was paying for Izzat's baby part of your Animal Charity Fund?
MADIHA	No, that woman is lying. Devraj?
DEVRAJ	*Chowkidar!!*
SONYA	You bought Izzat's baby to destroy evidence.
MADIHA	It was alive… the baby was alive.
SONYA	They sold you their dead babies.
DEVRAJ	I want you to leave… now!
MADIHA	They brought dead *animals.*
SONYA	You are destroying evidence of murder!
DEVRAJ	To hell with your evidence!
MADIHA	The evidence? The evidence is right here, right inside me. *(to SONYA)* I breathe more "poison" than any of those women in the slums. If what you say is true, then my baby must be ten times more deformed.
SONYA	You're damn right, madam, because the company's poison does not discriminate.
MADIHA	Then I'll be a good test case for you.
SONYA	What?
MADIHA	Sign me up for your study. Why not?
SONYA	My study is banned.
MADIHA	I offer my womb regardless.

DEVRAJ	What's wrong with you Madiha?
MADIHA	I'm helping you. I want to shut her mouth. *(turns to SONYA)* To see you posturing *(imitating her)* "I have this evidence, I have that evidence!" Well *(pointing at her own stomach)* here is my evidence. When my baby is born, you'll see.
SONYA	*(to MADIHA)* I won't be around. *(turns to DEVRAJ)* But how are *you* going to live with it?

SONYA exits. DEVRAJ turns to MADIHA.

DEVRAJ	What the fuck is wrong with you?
MADIHA	For the last two months, I have been thinking about how to break the news to you.
DEVRAJ	What news?
MADIHA	I missed two months.
DEVRAJ	What does that mean?
MADIHA	Yes, yes! I'm pregnant. Aren't you going to say something?
DEVRAJ	How did this happen?
MADIHA	Is that all you can say?
DEVRAJ	That night was the only night.
MADIHA	Are we talking about a single night? Devraj, I just revealed to you the fruit of our relationship.

They speak over each other.

DEVRAJ	I thought we had/
MADIHA	I'm going to be the/
DEVRAJ	an understanding.
MADIHA	mother of your child.
DEVRAJ	What do you want me to say?
MADIHA	Say something nice.
DEVRAJ	Are you sure?

MADIHA	Aaaaah…
DEVRAJ	Please, how do you know for sure?
MADIHA	I'm hungry, I vomit—of course I know for sure. It's in my body for goodness sake.
DEVRAJ	How long has it been?
MADIHA	Stop talking to me like that.
DEVRAJ	Madiha I think maybe—
MADIHA	What?
DEVRAJ	You could get an abortion.

> *MADIHA slaps him.*

MADIHA	No. No! I would never do that. Never. Not on my life! This is your baby for God's sake, Devraj!

> *Sound of escaping gas starts, which DEVRAJ notices but ignores.*

DEVRAJ	I'm sorry, I didn't know how to react to news like that.
MADIHA	Hold me in your arms, kiss me.

> *He kisses her.*

DEVRAJ	It's just that I don't want to do something now that I can't handle later.
MADIHA	You can't handle a baby?
DEVRAJ	What if the baby…
MADIHA	What?
DEVRAJ	I mean…
MADIHA	What? Is not healthy? Like the babies of those slum women?
DEVRAJ	I mean I'm not prepared to be a father.
MADIHA	Why wouldn't the baby be healthy?
DEVRAJ	I didn't say that.
MADIHA	What is that woman's research about?

DEVRAJ	Her research is nonsense. The slum mothers are not dying of diseases caused by Carbide Thunder, but by poverty. I don't give a toss about Labonté, I'm just nervous at the thought of being a father. Afraid of your motherhood out of wedlock! Afraid of mud slinging! What will everyone say? How will you handle that?
MADIHA	I'm sorry I doubted you, but I only wanted to help you.
DEVRAJ	By betting your baby with that dreadful doctor?
MADIHA	I believe so much in your work, I don't mind betting my womb to shut her mouth.

> *DEVRAJ holds her in his arms, kisses her.*

DEVRAJ	Oh Madiha you don't understand…

> *Deafening thunder starts.*

(looking out) What the hell is that?

> *Sound of thunder rises like a massive earthquake. Sparks start going off in all directions. DEVRAJ's phone starts ringing. Increasing sounds of chaos. People running in all directions. The noise from the street turns into cries for help. DEVRAJ runs to the window.*

DEVRAJ	God! The plant is burning…
MADIHA	Oh my God.
DEVRAJ	*(calling)* Rishi, Ashraf, Pooja! Wait! Wait! *(to MADIHA)* Go with them. Take the southeast exit. The southeast exit! *(calling out)* Raja! You stay here with me.
MADIHA	Aah! My eyes. I can't breathe.

> *MADIHA runs back to DEVRAJ.*

DEVRAJ	Cover your eyes, Madiha. Just run. Madiha, just GO!!! *(calling out)* Pooja, Rishi, help her!

> *He pushes MADIHA to escape. Complete darkness. We hear people whisper in the darkness.*

What in God's name has happened? What do you mean exploded? What tank?

JAGANLAL   What?

DEVRAJ   The MIC?

> *"Zahreeli Hawa" song starts, and continues overlapping all that is being said on the stage.*

SINGER   Khamosh cheekho say bhari
Yeay kahan say utha rahi hai aisi dardili hawa
Gaib say chalnay lagee jub
Ek Zahreeli Hawa.

MADIHA   My eyes.

JAGANLAL   Say it again. Where?

IZZAT   Run, *juldi, juldi chandalika bhago.*

MADIHA   I can't see anything.

IZZAT   Run, *chandalika,* run.

> *Loud clearing of throat is heard. It's from ANDERSON. We see him in the US, while people continue in whispers.*

ANDERSON   Sorry, I've had the flu for a week. But I'm getting over it. Washington is damp as hell at this time of year. I wanted to get back to Connecticut. But Julie was invited to lunch with the First Lady. What! How many? Over sixty?

> *Noise of a crowd in India.*

SONYA   Oxygen. Amylnitrate.

DEVRAJ   Mr. Minister, sorry to bother you.

SONYA   Thiosulphate.

ANDERSON   That's worse than Mexico!

SONYA   Oxygen. What do you mean you don't have any?

DEVRAJ   Damn it, Mukund, what about the scrubber?

JAGANLAL   Mr. Prime Minister, there is a problem…

MADIHA   Get out of my way! Move!

DEVRAJ   Move Mukund!

ANDERSON in the US.

ANDERSON   Who's our guy over there? The minister. I want to talk to him.

JAGANLAL   Carbide International's slogan has come to haunt us.

SONYA   Body number on the forehead. One thousand five hundred and thirty-eight. One thousand five hundred and thirty-nine.

ANDERSON   What do you mean, no one knows for sure what happened?

JAGANLAL   Why Bhopal? Why Bhopal?

As a deadly calm sets in, lights start to fade in. We see ANDERSON and JAGANLAL in their respective countries, which takes us to the next scene.

Scene 11

ANDERSON and JAGANLAL answer questions: JAGANLAL addressing the press in India and ANDERSON in the US. (In effect, they are talking to each other through the press.) A tightly packed crowd stands at some distance away from them.

ANDERSON   You're ten times safer inside a Carbide International factory than in a slum.

JAGANLAL   Right, they all died on the streets, no one died inside the factory.

ANDERSON   Gentlemen, if any of you have been to India, you know how they live over there. They are desperate for jobs. There was no slum around the factory when we started.

JAGANLAL   What rubbish. Slums were there long before the factory. Not just the slum, the Deputy Inspector General of Police's bungalow too.

ANDERSON   Look, the name of the game is not to nail me down;
            the name of the game is to provide for the victims.
            What they need is fair compensation.

JAGANLAL   That's so typical, so bloody typical of the West. The
            courts of India haven't even opened the case against
            him, and he's already telling us what's fair! Absconder
            of justice, that's who he is! Three deadlines have
            passed, Mr. Anderson, and you're still talking to the
            American press for a crime committed in India.

ANDERSON   I'm going to see to it that the suffering is adequately
            compensated; I will pay compensation—no question
            about that at all. But no, I don't think there is any
            criminal responsibility here!

JAGANLAL   Really? What do you think?

ANDERSON   Obviously I didn't have, I don't have, and I never will
            have a criminal intent! I am personally going to go to
            India to better understand the situation.

JAGANLAL   Thank you.

Scene 12

            *SONYA's makeshift clinic. Scores of victims are lying
            on the floor. IZZAT is among them. Many victims
            have eye patches. SONYA brings a patient in.*

SONYA   If you are sick, stay in this area. There are doctors here
            who can help you. If you're looking for someone, go
            behind the market square, by the lake… there's a big
            poster on the lawn that says "Unidentified dead." Go
            there first. *Wahan jauw.*

IZZAT   Doctor Sonya.

SONYA   What?

IZZAT   My body aches. What will happen?

SONYA   I don't know.

IZZAT	You know, *doctorni sahiba*. You have my file.
SONYA	The situation is changing every day. We're waiting for medicine. I have nothing here.

> *IZZAT pulls out a handful of tablets.*

SONYA	M & Ms?
IZZAT	I want to live, *doctorni sahiba*... stop this pain.
SONYA	Oh God, who sold you these?

> *SONYA throws them away. Song starts while SONYA keeps helping IZZAT. IZZAT coughs up lumps of blood and tries to stop the blood by shoving the edge of her scarf into her mouth. IZZAT convulses. SAUVÉ enters meanwhile.*

SINGER	Kaisa bhabhka kaisi gandh Ho rahi hai sans bandh Roshni ankhon ki mand Jismo jan main bus rahi hai, kaisi matmaili hawa Gaib say chalne lagi jub, ek zahreeli hawa
SONYA	Izzat, no!
SAUVÉ	Dr. Labonté.
SONYA	I can't talk to you now. Help me get her on to the table.

> *SAUVÉ hesitates.*

Help me!! She's got fluid in her lungs!

> *SAUVÉ and SONYA help IZZAT on to the table.*

SAUVÉ	Legally you can't help this woman.

> *SONYA continues to help IZZAT.*

If something happens to this woman, you'd be personally liable.

SONYA	There is a bag on the table. Get me a bronchodilator!
SAUVÉ	I don't know what that is. You shouldn't be here, doctor.
SONYA	It's grey plastic!

SAUVÉ	It's not safe to stay here. *(He looks for it, holds it up.)* Is this it?

SONYA administers a shot from the ventilator.

SONYA	Get me a rag.
SAUVÉ	You're on your own, Labonté.
SONYA	Attendant!!

SONYA keeps helping IZZAT. SAUVÉ leaves.

Scene 13

Amid sounds of protest, ANDERSON arrives in India. JAGANLAL receives him at the airport.

ANDERSON	Mr. Minister, I am so sorry.
JAGANLAL	Yes, Mr. Anderson.
ANDERSON	I really am sorry.
JAGANLAL	You don't have much time, Mr. Anderson.
ANDERSON	And I do appreciate your coming in person to meet me.
JAGANLAL	They are outside.
ANDERSON	Who?
JAGANLAL	The police.
ANDERSON	Am I being arrested?
JAGANLAL	You need protection.
ANDERSON	Where is Mr. Sarthi?
JAGANLAL	Well-protected!
ANDERSON	May I see him?
JAGANLAL	You will.
ANDERSON	Is it a police escort waiting for us?

JAGANLAL	Don't worry about the photographers. Let them photograph you. Our people need to see you answering to authority. I'm doing you a favour. I will keep you under house arrest. Twenty-four-hour surveillance. Nobody will be allowed near you but Sarthi. That is the best I can do under the circumstances.
ANDERSON	I'm sure.
JAGANLAL	*Chalo.*

Both exit.

Scene 14

JAGANLAL's office.

JAGANLAL	Doctor Labonté, we need your help.
SONYA	Pardon me?
JAGANLAL	The people of Bhopal need your help.
SONYA	You need my help? It's a little late. There isn't much I can do now. If you had listened to me earlier, if you had read my research, Mr. Minister. If—You're unbelievable. You're as bad as they are.
JAGANLAL	Doctor Labonté, I am asking you to please stay in Bhopal. I'd like you to work at the Hamidiya Hospital.
SONYA	You want me to care for—to give palliative care to the victims of this goddamn disaster that you, *you* are directly responsible for. We have no supplies, no oxygen, we are using the same syringes over and over again, we have no antidote for Carbide's—
JAGANLAL	What do you need?
SONYA	Thiosulfate. Sodium thiosulfate for a start. For the cyanide poisoning.
JAGANLAL	I'll see to it that you get all you need. Please write it down for me.

SONYA	You'll understand if I don't fall over with gratitude.
JAGANLAL	I am grateful to you.
SONYA	What is this about? What do you want from me?
JAGANLAL	I want you to continue the work you've been doing.
SONYA	The work?
JAGANLAL	Your research.
SONYA	The research you dismissed two weeks ago. The research you banned.
JAGANLAL	The situation has changed Doctor.
SONYA	I can continue my research without interference?
JAGANLAL	Yes. Yes.
SONYA	And if I agreed to continue my study, how do I know what will happen to my findings?
JAGANLAL	As I said, the situation has changed. I am in a position to make your findings public. To let the world know.
SONYA	Montreal. You're going to the trade talks, the conference. You can present the material there.
JAGANLAL	Yes. Yes I can, doctor.

Scene 15

ANDERSON at DEVRAJ's, under house arrest. DEVRAJ is sitting nearby.

ANDERSON *(on the telephone)* Yeah, how's the big snowstorm in Connecticut? Overnight? That makes me feel a helluva lot better. Oh no, beautiful, fine, fine, well, apart from being jet-lagged and under house arrest. What? Yes... I don't know.... What? That much? ...No. No. Fine. Get back to me. *(hangs up, turns to DEVRAJ)* We've lost eight hundred million in market capitalisation in the last week; production is shut down worldwide, so we have no revenue; and our insurance may not cover us. What do you people get up to in this country? *(tosses a safety manual at DEVRAJ)* What is this?

DEVRAJ   Your safety manual.

ANDERSON   Our safety manual? Did you ever look at it?

DEVRAJ   Yes.

ANDERSON   You had a total of four safety devices. How many were working?

DEVRAJ   The refrigeration was turned off at your request to cut costs. The flare tower was shut off to cut costs. The scrubber had just been repaired, but still didn't function. The water hoses did not reach the tower.

ANDERSON   The book says at least two should have been working. How many were working?

DEVRAJ   They were certified.

ANDERSON   But were they working?

DEVRAJ   I don't know.

ANDERSON   You don't know?

DEVRAJ   None!

ANDERSON   Who certified them?

DEVRAJ   The minister's safety inspection team—we were *certified.*

> DEVRAJ gives ANDERSON a logbook. ANDERSON flips pages.

ANDERSON   When was the last time they were certified?

DEVRAJ   Two weeks ago.

ANDERSON   When is the next certification?

> DEVRAJ is silent.

Okay... if the plant hadn't blown up, when would the next one have been?

DEVRAJ   Two weeks from today!

ANDERSON   That means week four. But that's already been certified.
             So have weeks six, eight and ten. What is going on
             here? You have clearance for periods that haven't even
             arrived yet?

DEVRAJ   This is India.

ANDERSON   My apologies, I didn't know.

DEVRAJ   We have to adjust to local conditions here.

ANDERSON   Which means?

DEVRAJ   We must bribe. There are only two certification officers
             for the whole state and they won't come every two
             weeks. So once they come for certification, we pay
             them to certify three months in advance. Corruption
             is culture here, sir.

ANDERSON   You had gas leaks before didn't you?

DEVRAJ   Not this big.

ANDERSON   What was done?

DEVRAJ   We handed out flyers door to door.

ANDERSON   Flyers? Aren't people illiterate? *(DEVRAJ doesn't
             answer.)* How much did you save shutting down the
             refrigeration?

DEVRAJ   It was—

ANDERSON   And the scrubber!

DEVRAJ   Listen sir—

ANDERSON   And on bribes… how much?

DEVRAJ   Mr. Anderson—

ANDERSON   Why wasn't I informed?

DEVRAJ   You were, sir. I have them recorded. Twenty-seven
             memos were sent to you.

ANDERSON   Twenty-seven memos?

DEVRAJ   Twenty-seven dead babies.

ANDERSON   What?

DEVRAJ	No, I'm sorry, eighteen, I sent you eighteen memos.
ANDERSON	How do I save this corporation?
DEVRAJ	We responded to all instructions sent by the head office.
ANDERSON	Just shut up.

ANDERSON picks up the newspaper.

This reporter here, Raj Kumar Keshwani, I keep seeing his name all over the place, how come he prophesied so much about the safety of the plant and I never heard about it?

DEVRAJ	Sir, he's been writing those ever since the plant opened.
ANDERSON	He mentions some clinic's research—about Carbide killing unborn babies!
DEVRAJ	A Canadian NGO doctor. She was doing research claiming that Carbide International has been poisoning unborn babies ever since its Bhopal plant was built.
ANDERSON	And you ignored it?
DEVRAJ	We had her barred from the plant.
ANDERSON	And what's this about a Carbide employee? Madiha Akram who is apparently pregnant with the CEO's child?

DEVRAJ snatches the newspaper from him.

So you got an employee pregnant.

DEVRAJ	Yes.
ANDERSON	What a mess. I thought I sent India a man with a vision. I didn't know I was sending a fucking playboy.

ANDERSON pushes a flyer in DEVRAJ's hand.

What does it say?

DEVRAJ	*Zinda nahi murda.*
ANDERSON	Which means?
DEVRAJ	"Dead not alive."

ANDERSON   "Wanted. Anderson. Dead not alive!"

DEVRAJ   I'm sorry Mr. Anderson.

ANDERSON   People are calling me the ghost of Bhopal. Look at
            these eyes—a total of nine hundred and two wrinkles
            under these eyes. Each wrinkle represents a Carbide
            plant somewhere in the world. I and my men and
            women have hung on to a single hope—that Carbide
            would be a good citizen in each of those nine hundred
            towns, and, as in Bhopal, would help to put an end to
            poverty. Help realise untapped potential. And you Mr.
            Sarthi, have killed that hope. All nine hundred of us are
            fighting for our lives. Carbide is fighting for its life.

DEVRAJ   Mr. Anderson, the courts have not decided anything
            yet.

ANDERSON   Corporations don't lose in courts, they lose under
            public scrutiny. *(giving him the flyer)* Merry fucking
            Christmas, Mr. Playboy.

Scene 16

> *The Hamidiya Hospital. Victims lying on the floor
> in groups. IZZAT and MADIHA are among them.
> MADIHA's eyes are covered with eye patches. IZZAT
> has one eye patch. IZZAT is nibbling dry seeds.*

IZZAT   Madiha *memsahib*? *(no answer)* Bai? Memesahib?
            Madiha *memesahib*? You don't talk. Not a word. Eh.
            (MADIHA starts to cough. IZZAT offers her seeds.)
            Would you like to eat? A little bit. Not even for the
            baby? *(passes grain to MADIHA who drops it)* Now you
            know where it is. You are saving it. You will need it
            later. Want to hear a story? Listen...

            (song) Aise kihis bhagwan
            Badd devta patta pay bathis
            Haath la mal kay nikalis maile
            Maile say janmis ek kauwa

Kauwa la kihis bhagwan
Ja tai khoj key bhumi la laan
Aise kihis bhagwan.

Pher kauwa, makdi, auo kekda mun kachwa kay
ghench la dabais,
Tub kachwa ha bhumi la ugal dees.

Paani ooper ghoom-ghoom kay
Jaal bicha dis makdi
Jaal kay ooper bade jatan say
Bhumi jama dis makdi
Bhum la pahchan
Aise kihis bhagwan.

Pher sab jan milkay nachay gaye bur bhidgay. Okhar
baad badd devta apan mudi kay jata say baal noach kay
phakis. Okhar say pade bun gaye. Udi pade la kaat kay
hul banis. Jub hul chale la lagagay taub bhumi say anna
upjis.

Anna la deemak kay banbee kay bheetar
Rakh do bhaiya
Sub munsay kay kaam yay aahi
Bolo ram ramiya
Kauwa, makdi, kekda, kachwa
Sab jan khais dhan.
Aise kihis bhagwan.

MADIHA   Phir kya hua?

IZZAT   Phir?

MADIHA   Yeah, what happened then?

IZZAT   Then the crop got infected by pests.

MADIHA   Then?

IZZAT   Then men began to search for chemicals to kill the
pests.

What happened next?

That chemical killed my daughter.

*SONYA enters. She shows signs of sickness due to the
poisonous gas.*

SONYA	*(to IZZAT)* She's talking?
IZZAT	Yes.
MADIHA	Sonya Labonté? Dr. Sonya Lab

> *MADIHA sits up, attempts to .*

SONYA	No, don't take that off.
MADIHA	Thank you. I know I have not been kind to you. I feel embarrassed.

> *SONYA examines her with stethoscope.*

SONYA	Don't be. Breathe.
MADIHA	I don't know how to thank you for giving me back my life… and my little baby.
SONYA	There is a heartbeat.
MADIHA	See, I told you.
SONYA	Yes, yes.
MADIHA	I need to see Devraj.
SONYA	Miss Madiha, there are some things you need to know. Bhopal is being littered with deformed and stillborn babies.
MADIHA	That won't include my baby. No. Look, those women lie. They lie about everything… about their animals… about their families… about their babies…
SONYA	Miss Madiha—
MADIHA	Like Izzat. She lied about everything—her dead dog, her dead pig, her dead goat…
SONYA	The chemical that killed Izzat's goat, killed her daughter; the same gas that poisoned you—is going to affect your baby.
MADIHA	I see what you're doing. You cannot stop, can you? You want to blame Devraj for everything. Why are you trying to scare me? Have you no shame?
SONYA	There was a baby born without eyes.

A   Why do you talk like that?

YA   I urge you to seriously consider terminating this
           pregnancy. I will not tell you what to do. I can't. But
           you need to know the facts.

> SONYA starts to exit. She coughs and staggers as she
> walks. She stops, gasps for air, and then collapses
> slowly as the lights close on her. Dr. Labonté dies.

Scene 17

> ANDERSON at DEVRAJ's house arrest.

JAGANLAL	This is the settlement you are proposing?
ANDERSON	Yes.
JAGANLAL	This is not just.
ANDERSON	Mr. Minister, there is always an element of speculation in these arbitrations. The point is—the dead have stopped dying.
JAGANLAL	What?
ANDERSON	The dead have stopped dying.
JAGANLAL	The dead have stopped dying?
ANDERSON	Look—
JAGANLAL	My people are dying faster than the insects your chemical was supposed to kill.
ANDERSON	Well, your casualty numbers don't match ours.
JAGANLAL	Two hundred thousand and counting.
DEVRAJ	There have only been two thousand recorded deaths.
JAGANLAL	Only?
DEVRAJ	We ought to be precise about the numbers.
JAGANLAL	Thirty-seven wards are affected.

DEVRAJ	That's the entire city.
JAGANLAL	And the poison clouds are not clear yet.
ANDERSON	Mr. Minister, we'll provide compensation. We'll look after the gas victims, but first of all, you have to determine how many.
JAGANLAL	What?
ANDERSON	Who was living in the affected wards at the time?
JAGANLAL	And how should I determine that? Should I go to every dead body and ask his home address?
ANDERSON	Well, don't you have census records?
JAGANLAL	As if they had homes.
ANDERSON	So what are we supposed to do? Pay for every patient you happen to have in your hospitals.
JAGANLAL	*(raising a file)* Three hundred fifty thousand registered medical files, two hundred thousand temporary disabilities, one hundred fifty thousand possible permanent disabilities.
DEVRAJ	How many of them are faking?
JAGANLAL	How does one fake death, Mr. Sarthi?
DEVRAJ	Half the dead wouldn't have been alive in the first place, had it not been for the wealth the plant provided.
JAGANLAL	For goodness sake, Devraj, I bent over backwards to grant you the People's Progress Zone. Bent over backwards to give you concessions that are unmatched in the history of India. You could at least think a little before opening your mouth *(imitates him in repulsion)* "Half the dead wouldn't have been alive!"
DEVRAJ	I'm sorry, Mr. Minister. You go on forgetting this was an accident!
JAGANLAL	An accident?

DEVRAJ   Do you think we'd do it purposely? It was an
                accident—a chemical, a chemical got too hot and
                exploded.

JAGANLAL   What chemical?

DEVRAJ   What?

JAGANLAL   Spell the name.

ANDERSON   What?

JAGANLAL   Spell that chemical, Methyl-Isocyanate. It decomposes
                to hydrogen cyanide and carbon dioxide. It burns the
                skin, eyes, and respiratory membranes. It penetrates
                the skin and is lethal in very low doses.

ANDERSON   Look, Mr. Bhandari, our scientists know perfectly well
                what they—

JAGANLAL   MIC, the gas that killed my people!

ANDERSON   We acknowledge the damage this explosion has done.
                But it was an acc—

JAGANLAL   You knew you had a problem.

DEVRAJ   No!

JAGANLAL   No? Buying dead animals?

DEVRAJ   That was the Animal Charity Fund.

JAGANLAL   Charity?

ANDERSON   Mr. Minister, we have charities in all corners of the
                world. This was an accident. It could have happened in
                the US.

JAGANLAL   Then why didn't it? It didn't happen in the US because
                you don't store enormous quantities of MIC at your
                American factory. It didn't happen there because you
                have automated monitoring systems: you don't rely
                on your workers' noses to tell you when there's been
                a leak. It didn't happen there because you have extra
                safety measures in place—measures you didn't bother
                to install here.

                Long silence.

ANDERSON	I believe we all share the same philosophy—
JAGANLAL	Aaah, so there's a philosophy to killing people?
ANDERSON	*(to DEVRAJ)* Show him our figures.
JAGANLAL	Your figures?
ANDERSON	These are generous amounts and my final offer.
JAGANLAL	Shouldn't the courts of India determine what's final?
ANDERSON	I have shareholders, insurance companies—they are throwing Molotov cocktails at the factory in Stuttgart. The company's bonds are on credit watch. You have no idea of the scope of my problems.
JAGANLAL	Regardless of your problems, you can't be your own judge and your own jury. This happened here and an Indian court must settle this.
ANDERSON	If you want to wait that long—but your people need help, *now*! Give him our figures. Please just listen carefully.
DEVRAJ	Eight thousand per death, four thousand per partial permanent disability, and two thousand per partial temporary disability!
ANDERSON	Not in Rupees, in American dollars!
JAGANLAL	This is what an Indian life is worth?
DEVRAJ	These figures are based on the Indian standard of living.
JAGANLAL	How American, Indian boy!
DEVRAJ	You had nothing here. We brought you a world-class plant.
JAGANLAL	A world-class plant? I licensed you to manufacture mega-quantities of Carbide Thunder and agreed to an outrageous extension to the People's Progress Zone. Why? Because my country is poor. We are not competitive on the global market. We are *always* in the position of trying to catch up to *you*. But the price *we* pay for trying to catch up leaves us *victims* of your

progress, your technology, and your crimes against humanity.

ANDERSON We are not criminals.

JAGANLAL pulls out Labonté's research.

JAGANLAL Really? All right, you don't want to wait for an Indian court, fine, you will go to a US court. I will negotiate with this.

ANDERSON What's that?

JAGANLAL Dr. Labonté's research

DEVRAJ That can't be admissible.

JAGANLAL Because you purposely hid information?

DEVRAJ This is ludicrous.

JAGANLAL And coerced mothers to abort and bury deformed dead babies listed in this study.

DEVRAJ Oh, please.

ANDERSON Let him speak.

DEVRAJ Mr. Anderson?

ANDERSON You be quiet.

JAGANLAL *(reads the front page)* Significant amounts of MIC Methyl-Isocyanate, have been detected in the blood of pregnant women, causing birth defects, birthing abnormalities, and deformities. Carbide International manufactures this product. This study shows that, while long-term health-risks are not conclusive, Carbide International has increased the production and…

DEVRAJ A woman you charged with kidnapping has done this research!

JAGANLAL We have dropped the charges. She is now working in the Hamidiya Hospital, and I have decided to lift the ban on her study and have asked a special commission to examine her findings.

JAGANLAL starts to leave.

DEVRAJ   Mr. Minister?

ANDERSON walks towards JAGANLAL, motions DEVRAJ to leave. DEVRAJ leaves.

ANDERSON   Mr. Minister, perhaps there is one area of our settlement that we could actually begin to discuss in depth.

JAGANLAL   Yes, there is an area we may talk about substantially.

ANDERSON and JAGANLAL talk. They are very animated but their words are inaudible to the audience.

Scene 18

MADIHA at the clinic. DEVRAJ enters.

DEVRAJ   Madiha?

MADIHA   Just say hello.

DEVRAJ   Hello.

MADIHA   No, like when you would come bursting through my door Sunday morning, so full of life, "Hello Madiha," and run into my arms… "hellooo Madihaaa!"

DEVRAJ   *(trying)* Hellooo Madihaaa. I thought you died.

MADIHA   Me too.

DEVRAJ   It's my fault. I told you to run. If only you didn't run, it's my fault, all my fault. You ran right into the gas… I'm sorry, I'm sorry. *(pause)* Say something… something… just say it.

MADIHA   I love you.

DEVRAJ   No.

MADIHA   I love you.

She touches DEVRAJ, then kisses him passionately.

DEVRAJ	I have been thinking.
MADIHA	About what?
DEVRAJ	About us.
MADIHA	Yes?
DEVRAJ	I should go back to the US.
MADIHA	You should?
DEVRAJ	And you must come with me.
MADIHA	Yes. When? How soon can we go?
DEVRAJ	That depends.
MADIHA	On what?
DEVRAJ	What Jaganlal does with Labonté's research.
MADIHA	Labonté isn't in the picture anymore.
DEVRAJ	But do you have any idea what Labonté's research was about? Do you?
MADIHA	Some nonsense about the factory? About the factory!
DEVRAJ	What about the factory?
MADIHA	I don't know… about animals, women, babies. I don't know.
DEVRAJ	Why do you think we paid for all those dead animals?
MADIHA	It's beca… the Animal Charity…. Oh my God.
DEVRAJ	My nightmare is growing in your belly.
MADIHA	You lied to me.
DEVRAJ	It was a mistake.
MADIHA	You told me—
DEVRAJ	Can you forgive me?
MADIHA	Forgive you? Forgive you for what?
DEVRAJ	This baby—
MADIHA	Forgive you for your own baby?

DEVRAJ	Madiha, please understand me.
MADIHA	That night, I thought I'd die. I was running… I couldn't breathe… I couldn't see. I fell and my hand touched something. It was a dead body. Oh God, I had never touched a dead body before. I never prayed before but that night I prayed, "God save me and the life of my baby." I wanted to prove to myself that what you had told me before the accident was true.
DEVRAJ	Madiha, I'm sorry. It was a mistake. I didn't think this accident would happen until it happened. I thought I was doing something good. I thought I would be a bringer of prosperity. I really thought that. Now I look at you… Madiha, I'll make it all up to you. We can start over again in America.
MADIHA	What will America do for me? Will it give me back my eyes? Will it heal what's growing inside me?
DEVRAJ	What's growing inside you will have to be aborted.
MADIHA	Will have to be?
DEVRAJ	Madiha, I don't want to leave you alone.
MADIHA	So it's that simple. If I don't abort, I'm left alone.
DEVRAJ	That's not what I said.
MADIHA	Then why do you want me to abort this baby?
DEVRAJ	It's not a baby.
MADIHA	What is it?
DEVRAJ	You saw Izzat's baby.
MADIHA	I am not Izzat.
DEVRAJ	You don't understand.
MADIHA	What do I not understand?
DEVRAJ	Imagine how that creature would suffer. Every day would be a reminder of the mistake I made. Imagine if the child lived… knowing that his father… that I was responsible. I want us to be together. I want to marry you…

MADIHA   You have really mixed me up.

DEVRAJ   I really do want to marry you, Madiha. I know
that now.... But we can't... we won't last with such
a burden in our lives.

MADIHA   Labonté told me that all abortions in Bhopal will have
to be recorded. It's government regulation.

DEVRAJ   We will go outside of Bhopal.

MADIHA   Izzat was saying that a woman died a horrible death at
the hands of a doctor outside of Bhopal.

DEVRAJ   Don't be afraid, darling. Are we poor, uneducated clods
who would leave such matters to some two-cent clinic
outside of Bhopal? *(holds her hands)* Hans will take
care of you. I think you have made a good decision.

MADIHA   Stop—

DEVRAJ   We'll leave all this—

MADIHA   Stop please, I haven't made a decision... I want to
think about it.

DEVRAJ   Shussssh.... Sleep.... We need to sleep.

MADIHA   I haven't made a decision.

DEVRAJ   Shussssh.... You will see the sense of it in the morning.

> *MADIHA rests, her eyes closing with drowsiness.*
> *DEVRAJ sits besides her.*

Scene 19

> *ANDERSON on phone.*

ANDERSON   I thought we had an understanding. I don't have the
luxury of only having one thing to worry about. I'm
turning my attention to other things. I can't think
about Bhopal one hundred percent of the time.

My hands? My hands shake hands with heads of state and men at the White House. My hands provide for a million employees around the world and give scholarships to bright Indian students. My hands were trying to build the future of this country. My hands are clean. I was ten thousand miles away.

We both know your charges are absurd. Well, they'll have to find me first, and then they'll have to drag me into court. I've got a plane to catch. Good luck.

Scene 20

        Action takes place in three locations: at the Montreal Conference, at a graveyard, and at DEVRAJ's house arrest.

        At the Montreal conference where JAGANLAL is preparing for a speech…

JAGANLAL   Dear Delegates, good people of Canada, and business leaders of the world assembled in Montreal, *je veux vous dire*, I want to tell you, *il n'y a pas d'amour*, there is no love left in Bhopal. There are ten thousand sick babies. Dying babies, orphaned at birth. What can I do? Seek to lay blame? Cry for one baby? No. Do I mourn the dead? No. Sad as it may sound, I cannot afford to mourn for the dead. It's useless. Because we know that for every child that dies, a new baby is born. The time for mourning has past, we must now pave the way to the future.

        Song starts.

SINGER   Kya Zamin kya aasman
Ek kohra ek dhuan
Ek kayamat ka sama
Gaib say chalne lagi jab
Ek zahreeli hawa.

At the graveyard, where IZZAT is sitting by a mud grave with Zarina's empty basket beside her...

IZZAT   Doctor *sahiba*, Zarina died the day she was born. One leg, one arm, no fingers... there was nothing right with her. Her tiny little heart was like dried rubber... I could see it under her skin. Doctor *sahiba*, can you understand me? The night Zarina died, I saw her in a dream, standing. Looking like an angel. "Free me from my pain," she said. "Why am I like this? I am already dead...." That night I felt something had changed. I woke up and turned to look at her. She had stopped crying. *(takes out flower petals from the basket and drops them onto the grave)* She has peace. You have peace.

At DEVRAJ and MADIHA's, where they are under house arrest...

DEVRAJ   *(to MADIHA)* What are you thinking?

MADIHA doesn't say a word, walks away from him, then tears the airline ticket in two. DEVRAJ is stunned.

MADIHA looks at IZZAT, who is at a distance. IZZAT looks at MADIHA. Both women start walking towards each other and meet centre stage. MADIHA takes IZZAT's hand in hers. The women have resolute expressions of defiance.

The end.

GLOSSARY

Aadab: Greetings.

Aagu chal kay uhi dhan main kida lag gay: Then the same crop got infected by pests.

Achha: Okay (here it implies "really").

Bai: Dear lady.

Basti: Locality.

Chal bhag. Bhagwan kay ghar say: Get lost from God's house.

Chalo: Let's go.

Chalo raasta Napo: Hit the road.

Chote Muh bari baat: Big talk for a little person.

Chowkidar: Security guard.

Doctorni Sahiba: Madam lady doctor.

Dhela: Mud ball (here it implies "a penny").

Haan haan: Yes, yes.

Hut haramzaadi: Get lost you bastard.

Hutt, bhaag, hatt bhaag: Get away, get lost.

Ja. Ja. Juldi… juldi…: Go, go, hurry up.

Juldi, juldi Chandalika bhago: Hurry up Chandalika, run.

Maa ji: Mother.

Malik: Master or sir.

Mandir: Temple.

Mantri ji: Mr. Minister.

Meharbani: Kindness.

Meharbani sahib, …Bus isay bacha leejiy: Please sir, save this baby.

Pagdandi: Narrow mud-path.

Phir ka houise: Then what happened?

Phir Kya hua: Then what happened.

Pundit Ji: The priest.

Sahib: Sir.

Sandas: Toilet.

Tarak chai or Masala: Super hot tea or masala tea.

Teekhai, teekhai: Okay, okay.

Zinda nahin murda: Dead not alive.

"Ek Zahreeli Hawa," Scene 1, page 5

A poison wind began to blow
from a place unseen,
Fiercer than the wounded heart,
Filled with helpless wailing,
Louder than silenced screams.
What could unleash such a wind as this?
A poison wind began to blow
from a place unseen.

A poison wind began to blow
from a place unseen.
With it came a scarlet tide,
The stink of impending death,
A yellow shroud, a winding sheet.
A poison wind began to blow from a place unseen.

Scene 10, page 41

Filled with helpless wailing,
Louder than silenced screams.
What could unleash such a wind as this?
A poison wind began to blow from a place unseen.

Scene 10, page 44

An acrid smell like rotted flesh that
Seared all eyes and sealed them.
Submerged with its soiled breath,
A poison wind began to blow from a place unseen.

"Aise Kihis Bhagwan," Scene 16, page 51

So said the great God. One day, the Great God rubbed his hands together and out tumbled a clump of clay. When it landed, it cracked open like an egg. Crack! That is how Crow was born.

"Crow!" yelled the Great God.
Crow, who only saw the Great God's shadow, trembled with fright.
"Go create Earth!" ordered the Great God.

Crow ventured out, the voice of the Great God still ringing in his ears. On the way he met Crab and Spider, also born from clay, and they went to make Earth together for the Great God.

At last, near a vast ocean, they came upon Turtle. They caught Turtle by the head and gave it a quick twist. Off it came! Heuh! Out came earth from Turtle's gaping neck. Without stopping, Spider spun overtop the water a magnificent web, on which she then sprinkled the soil from Turtle's neck…. That was how Earth was created.

When they saw Earth, Crow, Crab, Spider and Turtle rejoiced in song and dance. The Great God was pleased and let fall to earth a lock of his own hair, and from that lock sprang a mighty tree.

Crow, Crab, Spider and Turtle chopped the tree down and built a plough from the wood. They ploughed Earth and sowed the rich, black furrows with seed. And so they came to grow and harvest crops.

So many crops. Where to store them? They searched their minds and scoured the countryside. And then it came to them. Where the mighty tree had once stood, termites had built their mound. A mound with space enough to spare! Crow, Crab, Spider and Turtle all shared crops. So said the great God.

SONGS IN HINDI

Scene 1, page 5

ग़ैब से चलने लगी जब
एक ज़हरीली हवा

दिल के फफ़ोलों से भरी
किस-किस के नालों से भरी
ख़ामोश चीख़ों से भरी
ये कहाँ से उठ रही है ऐसी दर्दीली हवा
ग़ैब से चलने लगी जब
एक ज़हरीली हवा

एक मौजे लहू आ रही है
मौत की जैसी बू आ रही है
कूबकू सूबसू आ रही है
अपनी बेरंगी में भी एक ज़ग पीली हवा
ग़ैब से चलने लगी जब
एक ज़हरीली हवा

Scene 10, page 41

ख़ामोश चीख़ों से भरी
ये कहाँ से उठा रही है ऐसी दर्दीली हवा
ग़ैब से चलने लगी जब
एक ज़हरीली हवा

Scene 10, page 44

कैसा भभक्का कैसी गंध
हो रही है साँस बंद
रोशनी आँखों की मंद
जिस्मो जान में बस रही है, कैसी मटमैली हवा
ग़ैब से चलने लगी जब, एक ज़हरीली हवा

Scene 16, page 51

ऐसे किहिस भगवान
बड़ देवता पत्ता पे बैठिस
हाथ ला मल के निकालिस मैल
मैल से जनमिस एक कौआ

कौआ ला किहिस भगवान
जा तैं खोज के भूमि ला लान
ऐसे किहिस भगवान।
              फेर कौआ, मकड़ी, अऊ केकड़ा मन मछवा के घेंच ला दबाइस,
              ता कछवा हा भूमि ला उगल दीस।
पानी ऊपर घूम-घूम के
जाल बिछादिस मकड़ी
जाल के ऊपर बड़े जतन से
भूमि जमादिस मकड़ी
भूमि ला पहचान
ऐसे किहिस भगवान।
              फेर सब झन मिलके नाचे गाये वर भिड़गे।
              अेखर बाद बड़ देवता अपन मूड़ी के जटा से बाल नोच के फेंकिस।
              अेखर से पेड़ बनगे।
              उही पेड़ ला काट के हल बनाइस।
              जब हल चले ला लगगे तब भूमि से अन्न उपजिस।
अन्ना ला दीमक के बांबी के भीतर
रख दो भैया
सब मनसे के काम ये आही
बोलो राम रमैया
कौआ, मकड़ी, केकड़ा, कछवा
सब झन खाइस धान
ऐसे किहिस भगवान।

फिर क्या हुआ?

फिर?

Scene 20, page 63

क्या जमीं क्या आसमां
एक कोहर एक धुआं
एक कयामत का शमां
ग़ैब से चलने लगी जब
एक ज़हरीली हवा।

Rahul Varma is a playwright, essayist and community activist. Born in 1952 in India, he moved to Canada in 1976. In 1981, he co-founded Teesri Duniya Theatre (Teesri Duniya means "third world" in Hindi), which is a professional, multicultural company that produces socially relevant theatre examining issues of cultural representation and diversity in Canada. Rahul became the company's artistic director in 1986. To advance the company's mandate, he launched the theatre quarterly *alt.theatre: cultural diversity and the stage* in 1998.

He made his first forays into English language with a series of one-act plays that included *Job Stealer, Isolated Incident* and *Equal Wages*. With *Land Where The Trees Talk*, in 1989, he turned his attention to the creation of full-length plays. His full-length works include *No Man's Land*, the radio drama *Trading Injuries, Counter Offence* and his most recent work, *Bhopal. Counter Offence* has been translated into French as *L'Affaire Farhadi* and Italian as *Il Caso Farhadi. Bhopal* has been translated into French under the same title and has also been translated into Hindi and Urdu by India's pre-eminent director Habib Tanvir under the name *Zahreeli Hawa*.

Rahul lives in Montreal with his wife, Dipti, and his daughter, Aliya.